ACPL ITEM
DISCARDED

P9-EDX-865

OCT 31 '78

AFTER OLYMPIC GLORY

The Gold Medal of the Olympic Games

AFTER OLYMPIC GLORY

The Lives of
Ten Outstanding Medalists

by Larry Bortstein

illustrated with photographs

Frederick Warne
New York • London

Copyright © 1978 Larry Bortstein

All rights reserved. No part of this book may be reproduced or transmitted in any form
or by any means without permission in writing from the Publisher, except for brief
quotes used in connection with reviews written specifically for inclusion in a magazine
or newspaper.

Frederick Warne & Co., Inc.
New York, New York

Manufactured in the United States of America

LCC: 76-6779
ISBN: 0-7232-6135-0

1 2 3 4 5 6 7 8 9 10

2020594

For those who have
climbed Mt. Olympus — and
touched the stars

CONTENTS

ACKNOWLEDGMENTS

The author received a considerable amount of help and cooperation in writing this book. Most notably, he would like to thank the subjects of the individual chapters, most of whom granted personal interviews. Assistance came from many other sources as well. The author wishes to express his appreciation for their part in making this book possible.

The list of people includes: Elin Albright, mother of Tenley Albright; Neil Amdur, sportswriter, *New York Times*; Hal Bateman, sports information director, U.S. Air Force Academy; Larry Batson, columnist, *Minneapolis Tribune*; Irv Brodsky, director of sports publicity, American Broadcasting Company; Bud Greenspan and his wife, Cappy Petrash, of Cappy Productions, master creators of sports documentaries, including the television series *The Olympiad*; Lenore Hershey, editor-in-chief, *Ladies' Home Journal*; Edwin Mosler and Sam Sloan, New York State Olympic Committee; C. Robert Paul, press director, U.S. Olympic Committee; Fred Stabley, sports information director, Michigan State University; Glenn Sundby, publisher, *International Gymnast*; Jim Wergeles, publicity director, New York Knickerbockers; and Lois Woodyatt, secretary to Dr. Benjamin Spock.

DATES and SITES
of the
MODERN OLYMPIC GAMES

Summer Games
I   Athens, Greece, April 6-15, 1896
II   Paris, France, July 2-22, 1900
III St. Louis, Missouri, August 29-September 7, 1904
IV   London, England, July 13-25, 1908
V   Stockholm, Sweden, July 6-15, 1912
VI   Scheduled for Berlin, Germany, in 1916; canceled due
     to war
VII Antwerp, Belgium, August 14-29, 1920
VIII Paris, France, July 5-27, 1924
IX   Amsterdam, Holland, July 28-August 12, 1928
X   Los Angeles, California, July 30-August 14, 1932
XI   Berlin, Germany, August 1-16, 1936
XII Scheduled for Tokyo, Japan, then Helsinki, Finland,
     1940; canceled because of war
XIII Scheduled for London, 1944; canceled due to war
XIV London, England, July 29-August 14, 1948
XV   Helsinki, Finland, July 19-August 3, 1952
XVI Melbourne, Australia, November 22-December 8, 1956
XVII Rome, Italy, August 25-September 11, 1960
XVIII Tokyo, Japan, October 10-24, 1964
XIX Mexico City, Mexico, October 12-27, 1968
XX   Munich, West Germany, August 26-September 10, 1972
XXI Montreal, Canada, July 17-August 1, 1976

Winter Games
I   Chamonix, France, January 25-February 4, 1924
II   St. Moritz, Switzerland, February 11-19, 1928
III Lake Placid, New York, February 4-13, 1932
IV   Garmisch-Partenkirchen, Germany, February 6-16, 1936
V   St. Moritz, Switzerland, January 30-February 8, 1948
VI   Oslo, Norway, February 14-25, 1952
VII Cortina, Italy, January 26-February 5, 1956
VIII Squaw Valley, California, February 18-28, 1960
IX   Innsbruck, Austria, January 29-February 9, 1964
X   Grenoble, France, February 6-18, 1968
XI   Sapporo, Japan, February 3-13, 1972
XII Innsbruck, Austria, February 4-15, 1976

Introduction

The Olympic Games are without doubt the largest sports spectacular in the modern world. There may be one or two events—a cross-country skiing race in Sweden, a swim across the Dead Sea—that attract more participants. There may even be one event that more people watch for an hour or two every four years—the World Cup final in soccer.

But no other event features 9,000 participants over a period of two or three weeks with live audiences that run into the millions and television audiences reckoned in the hundreds of millions. The cost of staging a modern Olympics is staggering. In 1976 the governments of Canada, the Province of Quebec, and the City of Montreal spent an estimated one billion dollars.

Many Olympic competitors train for four or eight or even ten years, hoping for a chance to participate in the Games. Those who finally get there would probably play as hard and as well even if no one were watching. Olympic athletes are often known to have an ambivalent view of the Games. They remember with warmth and enthusiasm the spirit of cooperation and friendship among the participants. But at the same time they deplore the politics of national rivalry and the commercial appeal that seem to predominate.

The Olympics are hardly a modern idea. Historians have determined that the first Olympics were contested in 776 B.C. in Greece. The Greeks admired both physical and intellectual perfection and believed that the ideal human being would have "a sound mind in a sound body."

The Greeks kept the Olympics going on a four-year schedule for hundreds of years. In fact, if the Games came up while a war was being fought, the war was temporarily halted for the traditional event. In the twentieth century, by way of contrast, the Olympics have been canceled three times because of wars.

In 394 A.D., the Roman Emperor Theodosius put an end to Olympic competition. By this time the Olympics had become more of a circus than an athletic competition, and the emperor felt they were too raucous and rowdy to continue. For the next fifteen centuries, there were no Olympic Games.

Then in the 1890s, Baron Pierre de Coubertin, a French aristocrat, campaigned for a revival of the ancient idea. Like the Greeks, he believed that physical education should be an integral part of general education. And he hoped to advance this view through the Games. He succeeded in getting them started again in 1896. Appropriately enough, the first modern Olympics were held in Athens, Greece.

The baron was enormously proud. "The Olympic movement," he said, "tends to bring together in a radiant union all the qualities which guide mankind to perfection."

Since the first modern Olympics, the Games have been held every four years except for 1916, 1940, and 1944—years which fell during the two world wars. The baron would certainly be amazed and shocked at how different today's

Games are from the "radiant union" he envisioned.

To begin with, he would be astounded by the size of the modern Games. In 1896, only 285 athletes competed. In 1976, counting both the Winter and Summer Olympics, there were 9,000 competitors. And the competitors were outnumbered by the newspaper reporters, television crews, and others who helped to report the Games.

The baron would also be surprised by the changing role of women. In ancient times women were not even allowed as spectators, and in the first renewals of the modern Games, they certainly were not allowed as competitors. Finally, at the 1912 Games in Stockholm, women made a token appearance—in swimming.

Above all, Baron de Coubertin would be appalled at how imperfect and *un*-radiant the Games now are. Controversy and intrigue have become as much a part of the Olympics as the great athletic performances. Participants are found to have cheated by using drugs or, as in one recent case, to have introduced a sophisticated electric device which told judges that a point had been made in a fencing match even when it hadn't.

The Olympics have also been debased on occasion by various disputes between nations. In 1972 a group of Israeli athletes was taken hostage by Arab terrorists, and eleven of them were killed. In 1976, a large group of African nations walked out to protest participation by a team that had played all-white teams from South Africa. To ignore politics is no answer, either, as organizers found when they insisted on holding the 1936 Olympics in the grim atmosphere of Hitler's Germany. Indeed, political disputes often seem to outshine the performance of the athletes, whose event the Olympics is supposed to be.

Perhaps the imperfection of the Games should not be so

surprising after all. Despite all the high ideals, the organizers of the Games as well as the participants are human and imperfect themselves. They are subject to the same pressures and foibles and errors in judgment as the rest of us. Still, many of the subjects in this book voice the sincere hope that the Olympics strive to approach its original humanistic ideal.

The ten athletes in these pages represent a cross section of American Olympic champions. Nine of them won at least one gold medal, thereby setting themselves apart from the great majority of participants—those left behind to find their satisfaction only in having competed, but not won. Most of the champions here participated in the individual events that predominate in the Olympics rather than in a team sport. Four are track-and-field athletes, four competed in other individual events (ice-skating, boxing, diving, and swimming), and two were members of winning teams (in basketball and rowing). They represent a span of eleven Olympiads. Benjamin Spock, for instance, competed in the 1924 Games, while Micki King and Vince Matthews performed in 1972—forty-eight years later.

The striking thing about the ten is how different they are from each other—in background, emphasis on values, goals. For some, participation in the Games was a beginning; for others, an ending. By and large, they remember their few weeks at the Olympics with pleasure. But in looking back, they each set a different value on the experience. Some have spent their lives ever since promoting amateur athletics or working as coaches and administrators. A few became professional athletes. Some left athletics behind and never looked back.

They remind us, too, that the life of any athlete is strenuous and exhausting. Micki King broke her arm during Olympic competition, but insisted on making still another dive before receiving medical attention. When Bob Mathias won a gold medal in the decathlon, his first words were, "I wouldn't do this again for a million dollars." (Four years later he did it again and won the medal again, but never did receive a million dollars.) Their experiences suggest that perhaps one characteristic of an Olympic champion is perseverance—even beyond the point that others would consider foolhardy.

Most noteworthy, perhaps, is the different shape the Olympic experience takes for each of these ten individuals with the passing of the years. Most Olympic participants are young, and they train and compete as if there were nothing in life beyond the day of their event. But once that day passes, each of the athletes sees it from a constantly changing perspective. For some, the moment of glory grows in importance as time passes. For others, it shrinks. Most of them, however, will agree that their day of Olympic glory is by no means a lasting guarantee of success in the years to come.

Gold medal form

Chapter 1

Micki King

When the Olympic Trials for swimming and diving were held in Detroit in 1960, a young woman from the nearby city of Pontiac was entered in the three-meter springboard competition. Seeing the older, more experienced divers soaring off the board with grace and confidence, the girl was frightened and didn't even want to try. Her coach persuaded her to go ahead, if only for the experience of competing against world-class divers. She finished twenty-ninth in a field of thirty.

The young woman was Micki King. The history of her long quest for the Olympic gold medal is one of the most interesting stories in sport. Two years after that first Trial, she graduated from high school and entered the University of Michigan where she majored in journalism. She also swam on a women's relay team and played goalie on the women's water polo team. She was so good as a goalie that she was picked to the All-America team as one of the best water polo players in the nation.

She also continued her diving under the direction of Dick Kimball, one of America's leading diving coaches. Micki learned to dive not only from the three-meter board (nearly ten feet above the water), but also from the ten-meter platform (a dizzying thirty-three feet high). Kimball forced her to do her dives over and over again. At first she was afraid of the high platform; but soon she came to enjoy the sensation of flying through the air.

"I've felt the fear, sure," she says. "But the thing about the heights that really thrilled me in the beginning was that by starting high I could stay airborne longer and do all the moves, the rotations and the twists—which is impossible from the lower board.

"But when you hit the water from that height, you hit with such force that your shoulders and upper arms turn black-and-blue, and it hurts for quite a while. Remember, you're going about forty miles an hour when you hit the water from ten meters."

In 1964, while a sophomore at Michigan, Micki got a second chance to make the Olympic team. She was twenty now, an age when most divers are reaching their peak. She had already won the U. S. championship and was expected to be one of the springboard divers to go to Tokyo.

Although she didn't finish at the bottom of the list as in 1960, Micki missed on too many of her dives and finished fifth — not high enough to make the team. This time, losing was a real disappointment.

She went back to the university and, in both her junior and senior years, won the U. S. three-meter diving championship. Now she looked forward to still another chance to make the Olympic team. She graduated in 1966, and that fall enlisted in the U. S. Air Force, which offered her a career and a chance to continue her diving training at the same time.

After completing Officers Candidate School and being commissioned as a second lieutenant, Micki was stationed at

On the team

the University of Michigan to work with the ROTC (Reserve Officers' Training Corps) there. She continued to train under diving coach Kimball, and had developed to the point where she invented her own dives—maneuvers no woman had ever attempted before.

In 1968 Micki was the overwhelming favorite in the Olympic diving Trials. She was old enough at twenty-four to be called "Mama Max" by the other divers. This time there was no disappointment. She achieved the highest scores and went to the Mexico City Olympics as the top-rated woman diver, a favorite to win the gold medal.

Diving is scored by a group of judges. Each dive has been assigned a "degree of difficulty" from 1.2 for the easiest to 3.0 for the most difficult. The judges award a performance score of one to ten on each dive. Then the performance scores are multiplied by the degree of difficulty and the diver gets the number of points that result. The total points for ten dives in the competition determines the winner.

After eight dives at Mexico City, Micki King was ahead and appeared to be on her way to the gold medal. But she couldn't afford any mistakes on the remaining dives.

"I knew the ninth dive, the next to last, was the crucial one," she recalls. "A reverse one-and-a-half layout. I had won meets on it, but it's very easy to miss. My last dive was always my bread-and-butter dive. I felt that if I could at least be tied for the lead going into the last dive, I'd win it. But I needed a good next-to-last dive."

She failed to get it. Disaster struck as soon as she left the board. Her takeoff was bad and she was spinning her layout too fast. In an attempt to correct herself she swooped down toward the board.

"I didn't realize I was close before I hit," she remembers. "Then, bam! When my left arm hit that board I thought it was the loudest sound I'd ever heard in my life. Somebody told me later that after I went under I pounded the floor of the pool with my fist. I don't remember that. All I remember at that moment was absolute anger."

She climbed out of the pool in shock. Her left arm was obviously injured and almost totally numb. Officials offered to tape it up, but that would have disqualified her for the tenth dive. She was determined to try a dive even if she had to fake it.

"I knew I couldn't win the gold medal anymore, but I thought I might still salvage third and get a bronze." The pain was excruciating. "I fell into a complete crunch," she recalls with a wince. "I got through every part of the dive — a reverse one-and-a-half somersault with one-and-a-half twists. But it wasn't anything close to being good enough."

There would be no medal for King. She finished the competition in fourth place and the gold went to another American, Sue Gossick. "My immediate reaction was anger at myself for blowing it," Micki says. "The disappointment didn't hit me until the next day when I saw the American flag go up at someone else's presentation ceremony."

Micki left Mexico City with a cast on her left arm. One of the two long bones in her forearm had been broken in the collision with the board.

The story might well have ended there. "I had promised myself to quit if I won the gold medal," Micki remembers. Now, having lost, she felt she was through with diving. She threw herself into her work, directing off-duty education programs at a base near Los Angeles.

Then in the spring of 1969 her life turned around once more. The indoor Amateur Athletic Union national championship meet was being held in Long Beach, only a few miles from Micki's apartment. She went to the meet as a spectator,

An Air Force career—and still diving

and found that just sitting and watching the other divers was an agonizing experience. "It was the hardest thing I had ever done in my life," she says. After the meet she talked to Dick Kimball.

"If you feel so strongly," he told her, "maybe there's still some diving left in you."

Micki thought about it and finally decided to get back into competitive diving and make one more try for the Olympic gold. Working out evenings in a pool in Long Beach and doing special exercises to restore the strength to her left arm, Micki began to prepare seriously for Munich. In June 1969, she entered the World Military Games, competing directly against men. This was the first time such direct competition had been allowed. She finished fourth in the springboard and third in platform diving.

In August, at the Santa Clara Invitational Meet in California—one of the major competitions on the aquatic calendar—King won both the springboard and platform events. The Air Force had so much faith in its young officer that it allowed her time between meets to return to Michigan for special training with coach Kimball. Micki repaid the confidence of her superiors by sweeping to one victory after another. She won the World University Games title, the International Invitationals, her tenth U.S. AAU crown, and the 1971 Pan-American Games title.

By 1972, Micki—newly promoted to the rank of captain—was diving better than ever. But she could not completely erase the memory of that painful dive at Mexico City. "I never did try that dive again," she admits. Instead, she had developed several new and equally difficult dives. "I knew I couldn't play it safe and win. Easy dives don't win gold medals."

She was twenty-eight now, an old woman in international

diving circles. Yet with her first effort in Munich, a forward two-and-a-half somersault, it was clear that Micki was on target for the championship in springboard. She handled every one of her dives dexterously, smoothly, and confidently.

Cheers rang out from the packed gallery as Captain King gave a tremendous performance, showing power and finesse. There were no big mistakes this time. Micki won her gold medal at last.

She vividly remembers the presentation ceremony, receiving the medal, and the playing of "The Star-Spangled Banner."

"I remember thinking how much I didn't want to cry—but crying anyway. I thought I was a little more hard-boiled than that, that the moment would get by me. But it didn't."

This time, retiring from competition was much easier. Micki gave up competitive diving permanently to pursue a new career as a coach. "The gold medal was the ultimate," she says.

Micki King was born July 26, 1944, in Pontiac, Michigan. Her father, an engineer, loved athletics and was particularly fond of swimming. Micki was introduced to aquatic sports almost as soon as she could walk. The King family spent vacations at nearby lakes, and the little girl soon learned to swim. When she was four years old, her father would hold her above his head in the water, then toss her skyward so she could somersault into the water. She loved the sensations of flying through the air and landing in the water.

Her sporting activities were hardly limited to the water. "I always thought of myself as being different—not at all the average kind of girl," she recalls. "I was a real tomboy. I loved all sports. I played softball and baseball with the boys, and they used to choose me before they chose any of the boys because I could hit the ball harder than they could."

Micki's parents were pleased that their only child was so athletically inclined. But they also realized that the boys would soon grow old enough to compete in organized school sports open to males only. Then Micki would be left out. So they encouraged her to find a sport she could practice on her own, an individual sport rather than a team-effort one.

Because ice-skating was popular in Michigan, Micki took classes in figure skating. Her natural athletic talent enabled her to master the fundamentals of the ice figures quickly. But she recalls her intense dislike of the sport.

"I tried it for a while, but I didn't like the routine. I still can't understand why I got bored with the routines of figure skating, but not with the routines of diving."

At the age of ten, Micki entered the world of diving at the local YMCA. The spring of a diving board gave her the same exhilarating feeling she had experienced when her father used to throw her in the air. Micki had found her sport.

It wasn't easy for her at first. "All the boys at the Y played 'follow the leader' on the board," she recalls. "The first time I followed them, I was scared. It was new, it was freaky. But it was also fun! For five years, I dived just for the fun I got out of it."

Her first plunge into competitive diving was a big success. She was only fifteen when the Y coach asked her to join the team for a meeting in Toledo, Ohio—and she was the only girl in the competition. She remembers being quite nervous and having a sick feeling in the pit of her stomach. Nonetheless, she won the event. "It was a squeaker," she recalls modestly. "I didn't realize how much more there was to it before I could be really good. I decided I had been lucky to win. From then on, that was it. I didn't want to be lucky. I started to practice as hard as I could to get as good as I could."

Micki's sports heroes at this time were men like Bobby Layne, the quarterback of the Detroit Lions; Al Kaline, the rightfielder of the Detroit Tigers; and New York Yankee superstar Mickey Mantle. Once her father cut out a newspaper picture of a top woman diver and presented it to Micki. "I still thought more about Mickey Mantle than I did about her," she admits.

Micki knew that her favorite athletes had succeeded because they were willing to devote themselves to their sports wholeheartedly. So she poured all her efforts into training. Soon she was working three long sessions a week with a high school coach who had previously coached only boys. So far, she had been able to get by doing the dives she enjoyed; now a lot more would be required.

Micki strived for the balance she knew was necessary. She had to learn to do the relatively simple dives flawlessly. At the same time, she would have to learn the more difficult and dangerous maneuvers. Her improvement was steady but unspectacular. She progressed from the low one-meter board on which all novices begin to the three-meter board, and finally to the ten-meter platform.

In 1960, after only a year of coaching, Micki went to the Olympic Trials in Detroit and finished at the bottom of the list. Then came her disappointments at the 1964 Trials, her broken arm and fourth-place finish in 1968, and finally her long overdue victory in 1972. Her persistence and good humor over these twelve years amazed and inspired a whole generation of younger competitors.

By the time she won the gold medal, Micki King was a captain in the Air Force. Her friends wondered how she would be able to continue her military career and still stay close to diving. The question was quickly answered.

Captain Micki King coaches Rich McAlister, 1975 Academy graduate

In early 1973 Micki was appointed diving coach at the Air Force Academy near Colorado Springs, Colorado—the first woman coach at any of the service academies. She took the new appointment in stride. "They needed a coach," she says, "and it would have been dumb of them to hire a civilian when they had me."

She also taught tennis, volleyball, gymnastics, and swimming to physical education students at the academy. Her male colleagues may have resented her presence sometimes, but they couldn't quarrel with her work habits or her success. She put in long hours, longer than almost any man on the athletic staff. And she soon became a winner as a coach. In her second year of coaching, one of her divers, Rich McAlister, captured the three-meter title in the National Collegiate Athletic Association championships.

Micki relished her successes but was impatient with people who were continually amazed at her accomplishments. "People keep asking me what I do coaching a men's team," she says. "My answer is, 'I've eliminated the locker room pep talk.' I hate to make an issue out of something I don't consider an issue. I've grown up in a man's world, I'm very comfortable with men, I can talk man talk."

The summer of 1976 ushered in two big events. First, the Air Force Academy welcomed its first women cadets. When the initial group of 150 arrived, they found one woman there to greet them and cheer them on. By this time Micki had been in the Air Force for nearly ten years. It had been a good career for her and she was happy that women now would have the same opportunities for education at the academy as men.

"Women have to meet the same physical and academic requirements as men," she points out. "I monitored many of the preliminary tests that were taken by the first-year applicants. It really was a thrill to see so many women looking for this kind of excitement in their lives.

"Of course, you always find some who don't quite understand what it's all about. One girl wrote me and asked what kind of modeling courses the academy offered! But most of the women coming in are prepared for the hard work and really want the training they'll get. This isn't the life for everybody, you know. All the cadets, the women as well as the men, have to do a tremendous amount of running and heavy physical exercise. But for women who really want the experience, it's a great challenge."

Those who opposed the admitting of women to the academy noted that a fair number of the first women cadets dropped out during the first summer. Micki points out that a fair number of the men drop out, too. In fact, the percentage of women dropouts in those first months was lower than that of the men.

The second big event that summer was Micki's marriage to Lieutenant Jim Hogue, who had graduated from the academy in June. The wedding came as a surprise to many—with good reason. The two had had to keep their romance a secret, to avoid all the gossip had it been known that a cadet was dating one of the few women faculty members.

Jim Hogue was a swimmer on the team who set academy records in several events; and he was captain of the team in his senior year. Since the swimming and diving teams practiced at the pool at the same time, Jim and Micki saw each other every day, acting very casually toward each other. Jim's life as a cadet was so busy that it was even hard for him to see Micki during his off-duty hours.

After graduating, Jim became a personnel officer at the academy. "I outrank Jim right now," Micki says with a smile.

Lieutenant Jim Hogue

"The rules require him to salute me when we meet during business hours or in public. He calls me Captain Hogue and I call him Lieutenant Hogue."

Early in 1977, the Hogues moved to Vance Air Force Base in Oklahoma where Jim had been accepted for flight training. Micki was assigned to the base to set up recreation programs for Air Force men and their families. For the time being, she was out of coaching and far away from the world of competitive diving.

The Hogues look forward to a joint career in the Air Force, and Micki hopes that one day both she and Jim will reach the rank of general. "Can you imagine two generals in the same house?" she asks with a laugh.

Wherever she goes and whatever she does, Micki King/Captain Hogue will take with her the qualities of determination and perseverance that she showed as a competitive diver. And the millions who saw her in Olympic competition will continue to admire her accomplishments—as a diver, as a woman, and as a human being.

"The Greatest"

Chapter 2

Muhammad Ali

Of all the famous people in the world—government leaders, kings and queens, movie and TV stars, and sports stars included—probably the most famous of all is the man who calls himself Muhammad Ali. It's an Islamic name like those of the people who live in Egypt, Iran, or Pakistan. He is black, the descendant of Africans, but American-born. He is a boxer, a heavyweight champion of the world. Millions of people who have never seen a boxing match know his name and admire him.

Who is Muhammad Ali and how did he gain worldwide fame? The answer is one of the most amazing stories in sports. And it all began at the Olympics.

In 1960 the Olympic Games were held in Rome, Italy. Among the athletes who lived in the specially constructed Olympic village was a young black fighter, Cassius Clay. He was to compete in the light heavyweight class, and was said to be a very promising boxer. He had already gained the championship of the most important amateur tournament in America, the Golden Gloves.

There was something special about young Clay. He was handsome, friendly, and talkative, and each day he would roam through the village, stopping frequently to greet and talk with athletes from other countries and take photos of them with his little box camera. He seemed amazed at the people he saw. Once he was talking with a reporter from the United States when a group of athletes from India passed by. "Excuse me," he interrupted the reporter, grabbing his Brownie. "I gotta take some shots of those guys with the beards."

In the ring Clay was all business. Olympic matches go only three rounds, so a fighter must quickly take control and impress the judges with his skills. In his first bout in the light heavyweight competition, he beat the Belgian Yvon Becus. Then he defeated Gennadiy Shatkov, a tough Russian, and Tony Madigan, one of the best fighters Australia had ever sent to an Olympics.

In the final bout for the gold medal, Clay was pitted against a huge fellow from Poland with the jawbreaking name of Zbigniew Pietrzykowski. Clay called him "Ziggy" for short. It was a bruising fight. "That Ziggy was a tough fighter," he admitted after the bout. "But you notice he looked all beat up and bloodied, and I don't have a mark on me."

Cassius had won the gold medal. In his remaining days in Rome, he even wore it to bed. "It was the first time I ever slept on my back," he remembers. "I had to, or the medal would have cut into my chest with its sharp edges. I was very proud to get it, and I was very proud to be an American and competing for my country."

At a press conference after winning the medal, a reporter from the Soviet Union asked Clay how he felt about conditions for blacks in the United States, especially in his hometown of Louisville.

Clay resented the question. "We've got a better country than you've got, and it's a lot better than Africa, where you have to fight off snakes and alligators," he said. That remark soon became an embarrassment to him. In later years he visited Africa often and came to realize that, as a boy, he had learned very little about that continent.

Soon after Clay came back from Rome, he visited New York City. About to turn professional, he began to make television appearances and talk to newspapermen. Wherever he went, he wore his blue Olympic blazer with "USA" embroidered across the front and his gold medal with the word "Pugilato" (Boxer) engraved upon it.

One day while walking near Times Square, a passerby approached him. "Aren't you Cassius Clay?" the man asked.

"Yeah, man, that's me," Cassius admitted with a grand smile. "How'd you know?"

"I saw you win the Olympics on TV," replied the man. "So did lots of other people. They all know who you are."

"Really?" Clay said. "Then I guess I *am* worldwide famous."

Cassius seemed to love the attention he received as the result of his Olympic victory. He would soon go on to even greater victories. But he would have some bitter disappointments along the way.

Cassius Marcellus Clay was born on January 17, 1942, in Louisville, Kentucky. His father, Cassius Marcellus Clay, Sr., was a sign painter; and his mother, Odessa Clay, worked as a maid. Mrs. Clay recalled that he was an unusually active and independent child from the very beginning.

Eighteen-year-old Cassius Clay jolts Russian boxer Shatkov in a bout in Rome, Italy

By the time he was twelve, Cassius was unusually strong and tall for his age, but he weighed a skinny 112 pounds. He played team games with his friends, though he was never especially good at them.

One day his father gave him a new Schwinn bicycle with red lights and chrome trim. Soon afterward, the boy rode the bicycle to the Louisville Home Show, an exhibition at which there was free popcorn and candy for youngsters.

It was raining heavily when he and his friends left the show. To his dismay, Cassius saw that his bike was gone. Angry and afraid of what his father would say, he ran up and down the streets in the rain searching for his bike. He couldn't find it. Someone suggested that he look at the nearby Columbia Gym, where policeman Joe Martin ran a boxing program for local boys.

Cassius found the gym building and burst through the door. Several young men were punching the heavy bags that hung from the ceiling of the gym and others were sparring with each other. But Cassius hardly noticed. He was crying.

Pouring out his sad story to Joe Martin, he blurted out, "If I catch the boy who took my bike, I'll whup him good."

Martin suggested that if he really wanted to "whup" someone, he should join the group at the gym to learn the skills of boxing. Cassius got his father's permission and began to come regularly.

Joe Martin was a demanding instructor. The young boxers ran for miles outdoors to build up their legs and their stamina. And they worked for hours in the gym, learning boxing techniques, sharpening their reflexes, and strengthening their muscles. Cassius trained hard and his skills began to develop. Martin soon saw that this young man had uncommon potential as a boxer. But he could not understand the young fighter's interest in the heavyweight division. Cassius would look at photographs of legendary former heavyweight titleholders like Joe Louis and Jack Dempsey and announce, "I'm going to be the next heavyweight champion." Yet the boy gave no indication that he would ever grow big enough to fight in the heavyweight ranks.

"I don't know what it was about heavyweights that impressed me," he later wondered. "Nobody on either side of my family ever grew that big, and most people figured I might end up as a middleweight, about 160 pounds, or a light heavyweight, one division below heavyweight. As a teenager, I was just as tall as I am now—about six feet three— but I was really skinny then."

In 1958 he entered the Golden Gloves tournament for the first time. Although he was only sixteen, he could already beat most of the fighters in his weight class. Then early in 1960 he captured both the national Amateur Athletic Union and the Golden Gloves championships. By now he was fighting as a light heavyweight and his victories made him a strong candidate for a place on the Olympic team. In the Olympic Trials, he battered a succession of opponents to win the spot. Late in August he flew to Rome with the rest of the boxing squad.

Cassius returned to the United States a hero. Back in Louisville, he was honored by the mayor and praised by the local newspapers. He soon learned, however, that he was still a second-class citizen in America because of the color of his skin. One night he went out with a friend, Ronnie King, whom he had known since boyhood. The two young men went to a cafeteria, sat in a booth, and ordered hamburgers and milkshakes. Cassius was still wearing the gold medal around his neck at the end of a red, white, and blue ribbon.

In those days many restaurants had separate sections for

black people. Others refused to serve them altogether. That night the owner of the place bellowed out, "We don't serve no niggers!" The waitress recognized Cassius and tried to explain who he was; but the owner shouted louder than before, "I don't serve no niggers. I don't care *who* he is."

The man's shouting attracted the attention of a young white motorcycle gang seated at the counter. When Cassius and Ronnie left in embarrassment, the white men left their seats and followed them. They were going to beat up "those niggers" to teach them a lesson. Cassius and Ronnie fought back and, after a few minutes of bloody action, succeeded in driving off the toughs. As Cassius wiped the dirt from his clothes, he did a lot of thinking. He thought of the man in the cafeteria and the gang he had just fought off. And he remembered the questions of the Soviet reporter at the press conference in Rome. Then he thought about the gold medal hanging around his neck. It wasn't really gold—the gold covering was already peeling off. And what difference had it really made to him? He still couldn't eat where he pleased or even live in peace.

Suddenly he jumped up and ran back to his car. He and Ronnie drove to the Jefferson County Bridge that spanned the Ohio River. He stopped at the middle of the bridge, got out, and went to the railing. Then he unfastened the ribbon on which the gold medal hung. Before Ronnie could stop him, Cassius dropped the medal, ribbon and all, into the river.

"I had to do it," he explained later. "That medal wasn't helping me get any respect like I thought it would. It was just an old piece of metal with a cheap raggedy ribbon. I had a big pain in my stomach from that whole night and everything that happened at the cafeteria and all. But after I threw the medal into the river, the pain went away.

Working his way up the boxing ladder

"I thought the medal would give me automatic fame and glory," he said. "I was wrong. The Games themselves were a great experience. It was what happened after the Games that screwed me up for a while. The medal couldn't do everything for me I thought it could."

He got rid of the gold medal, but he didn't give up boxing. A group of Louisville businessmen agreed to finance him while he worked his way up as a professional fighter. He put himself under the direction of Angelo Dundee, one of the great trainers in boxing. Soon he was fighting again—and winning. By this time he was indeed the heavyweight he had always wanted to be; now his goal was to become the heavyweight champion.

Clay found a new source of strength in the religion known as the Nation of Islam. One day as he was walking along a street in Miami Beach after a hard afternoon of training at Angelo Dundee's Fifth Street Gym, he saw a black man standing on a corner handing out copies of a newspaper to passersby. Cassius stopped to talk with the man and took a copy of the newspaper—*Muhammad Speaks,* the official publication of the Nation of Islam in the U.S.

He discovered that he shared many of the views of the Black Muslims, who believed that black people had to assert themselves and stop being ashamed of their race.

Cassius began to attend local meetings of a Black Muslim group and learned more about their faith. Their leader was Elijah Muhammad. They were Mohammedans who studied the teachings of the prophet Mohammed and worshiped one God whom they called Allah. For nearly three years, while working his way up the boxing ladder, Cassius kept his interest in the Nation of Islam a solemn secret from the rest of the world.

Clay attracted a great deal of attention for his exploits in the ring. He knocked out one opponent after another and finally got a chance to fight for the championship. His opponent was to be champion Sonny Liston, who was considered the most fearsome of all the heavyweights in history. He had murder in both fists and was an overwhelming favorite to defeat Clay.

The young man surprised everyone. He thoroughly outboxed, out-thought, and out-ran Liston. At the beginning of the seventh round, Sonny was so tired he was unable to rise from his stool in the corner of the ring. Cassius had scored a technical knockout and was the world's new heavyweight champion.

The next day the public was given another big surprise when Clay announced that he had become a Black Muslim. His name was to be Muhammad Ali. "And I want you to call me that from now on," he said.

The reaction to his announcement was extraordinary. Many whites and even some blacks believed that the Black Muslims were dangerous. Ali (as he preferred to be known) was attacked from all sides, by sportswriters and by boxing promoters. The world seemed to forget that he was boxing's newest and possibly best champion. Suddenly he was famous not for his boxing skill but for his religious beliefs. Muhammad Ali refused to back down. "I don't have to be who you want me to be," he said. "I'm free to be who I want."

During the next three years, Ali defended his heavyweight championship nine times, fighting brilliantly. And he continued to be a great showman, promoting his fights with great skill and humor. Most of those who came to see him fight, however, were rooting loudly for the other man. Millions wanted to see Ali get beaten.

Then in 1967 came another big test. Ali was drafted into the U. S. Army. The country was at war in Vietnam and hundreds of thousands were being drafted and sent there to fight. When the time came for Ali to enter the army, he refused. He claimed that he was a minister of the Black Muslim faith and that he deserved a deferment such as ministers of other faiths were given. But the courts had ruled against him. When he refused to go into the army, he was condemned as a draft dodger who would not support his country in time of war.

Boxing officials promptly outlawed Ali from the ring. Even though he was awaiting trial on charges of draft evasion, no state in the country would allow him to fight within its borders. And the federal government would not allow him to leave the country so that he could fight elsewhere.

Ali, only twenty-five years old, was probably at the peak of his form as a boxer. But for the next three years he was banned from the ring. In the meantime, ironically enough, his popularity increased. People who had been angry at his stand on the draft had now turned against the war. Ali became a popular speaker at colleges and universities. Outside the United States, where the war was very unpopular, he became a hero.

Finally, in late 1970, Mayor Sam Massell of Atlanta and Georgia State Senator Leroy Johnson joined forces to help Ali obtain a license and return to competition. There were threats from groups that disliked Ali, and, in the weeks before the fight, Ali found his own nervous tension mounting. But on October 26, 1970, he stepped into the ring in Atlanta's Municipal Auditorium and, in his first fight in forty-three months, easily disposed of Jerry Quarry in three rounds. Some weeks later, the United States Supreme Court ruled in Ali's favor. It said that he had qualified as a minister of the Black Muslim faith and that he had not broken the law when he refused to join the armed forces.

Could Muhammad fight his way back to the top? Only

time would tell. In March 1971 he faced Joe Frazier, who had become champion after Ali's forced ouster from competition. "Smokin' Joe" was the 1964 Olympic heavyweight gold medalist. In a classic brawl, Frazier won a decision over Ali after they had fought the maximum fifteen rounds.

Many people thought that Ali would retire then. But determined to prove that he was not washed up, he stayed in the ring. In 1972 he had six fights and won them all. He also traveled around the world to speak with leaders and meet the peoples of many nations.

In 1973 he lost another fight. A relatively unknown fighter, Ken Norton, broke Muhammad's jaw early in the fight and won by decision in twelve rounds. Ali had never been beaten so clearly before. But later in 1973, in a second fight, Ali did beat Norton; it was a split decision. From then on, with little difficulty, he continued to beat everyone else he faced.

By this time, young George Foreman, the Olympic heavyweight champion at Mexico City in 1968, had become the heavyweight champion of the world. Foreman had destroyed Frazier in two rounds to capture the crown. Before he could fight Foreman, Ali had to beat his old rival Joe Frazier. This time Ali won in twelve rounds.

Then came the championship. The fight was held in the African republic of Zaire. Ali went to Zaire weeks ahead and became a tremendous hero in the country on the Congo River. When he climbed up into the ring in the outdoor stadium, tens of thousands were chanting "Ah-Lee, Ah-Lee, Ah-Lee." He knocked Foreman out in the eighth round and reclaimed the heavyweight throne.

It was one of the most amazing comeback stories in all of sports history. And Muhammad is by all odds the most amazing of all boxing champions. By most accounts he is also the wealthiest, having won more than $30 million in the ring. In 1975 he addressed the senior class at Harvard University, the most prestigious university in America.

"I just barely graduated from Central High in Louisville with passing marks," Ali told them. "So you know what kind of an honor it is for me to get to speak at Harvard, an uneducated black man like me."

Few have ever doubted Ali's intelligence, even though he has always had difficulty with reading. In a newspaper, every word with more than two syllables stops him. He has to work at it. Because of this reading problem, Muhammad almost always delivers a talk—such as the one at Harvard—completely from memory.

By 1977 Ali was thirty-five, an age when boxers (and most other athletes) begin to lose to younger men. He threatened to retire several times, but then decided to fight once more. Soon he would be gone from the ring for good. He says of the millions he has earned, "That's more than enough money for any man. I want to do good with it for people less fortunate than me."

And in several cases he has stepped in to help. For example, early in 1976 in New York City, he came to the rescue of a home for the elderly that was threatened with bankruptcy. He arrived unannounced one afternoon, asked to see the director of the home, and presented him with a substantial check. The people in the home were perfect strangers to him. This kind of generosity mystifies people who don't know him. He always seems to do the unexpected, keeping both his friends and his enemies off balance.

Of course, Ali has also been known to treat himself well. His major passion has been automobiles. "I own more cars than suits," he admits, "because I like getting around in new cars all the time." Often he does his own driving. He hires

Ali and Dick Gregory warm up outside Ali's office after Ali urged support for Gregory's 1976 cross country food run

chauffeurs—and they end up riding in the back seat. When people recognize him and ask him how things are going, Muhammad jokes that things are so rough he's taking on a little part-time work as chauffeur. Pointing to the real chauffeur, he says, "That's the white boss in the back."

Muhammad always has maintained that he is "The Greatest." (In fact, that is the title of his autobiography.) Early in 1976, a poll of 500 sports editors, writers, and broadcasters confirmed that Ali is indeed "The Greatest." He was voted the greatest fighter of all time, ahead of Joe Louis, Jack Dempsey, and his boyhood idol, Sugar Ray Robinson.

The millions of people around the world who have been touched by him would have called such a poll unnecessary in the first place.

Mathias in motion—the youngest decathlon champion

Chapter 3

Bob Mathias

People around Tulare, California, still recall with awe the feats of a high school athlete named Bob Mathias. He was probably the finest scholastic athlete ever to compete in the state of California. In basketball, he was a skillful center. In football, he was an excellent running back. But it was in track-and-field that he truly shone. In his junior year he had already set high school records in the discus, high jump, and low hurdles.

By the time he turned seventeen, Mathias was six feet tall and weighed 190 pounds. With deep blue eyes, square chin, and wide shoulders, he was an extremely handsome and photogenic figure. In the spring of his senior year, college recruiters swarmed to his hometown with scholarship offers. Some wanted him to play football, some basketball.

But Virgil Jackson, the track-and-field coach at Tulare High had another goal in mind. Never before had Jackson had a student with such talent. He thought that Bob's all-around skills might lend themselves to the decathlon — the arduous ten-event test of an athlete. If Mathias trained conscientiously, Jackson thought, he might well win an Olympic medal in four years' time—at the 1952 Games.

One afternoon in May 1948, Jackson watched Bob win several events in an interscholastic meet. Afterward the coach suggested to Bob that he enter the decathlon in a regional Olympic Trial to be held in Pasadena in June. Mathias had never even heard of the decathlon. He had never pole-vaulted, thrown the javelin, or run 400 meters and 1500 meters in competition — four of the ten decathlon events! Nevertheless, he agreed to enter the meet.

In three weeks Jackson taught Mathias to pole-vault. It was a difficult skill for so big and muscular a fellow to master, but Bob had the talent as well as the desire. Jackson had no illusions that Bob would win the regional Trial; but it would provide an excellent opportunity for the young man to test his skills against a field of older, more experienced athletes.

Incredibly, Bob outperformed the entire field and won the Pasadena meet. He threw the discus 140 feet and long-jumped more than 21 feet. Even his best marks would not qualify him for an individual event. But this seventeen-year-old could do everything — the field events, the jumping events, the dashes — even the grueling 1500-meter run.

It was a stunning accomplishment for the youngster in his first competitive decathlon. But the weeks of heavy training were beginning to tire him. "The more I hear about de-cathlons," he said, "the less I like them."

It was hardly the time for Bob to stop. He had qualified for the national Trials, to be held in only two weeks. He might not have to wait until 1952 to make the U.S. Olympic team; he could make it in 1948. Coach Jackson urged Bob on in practice.

"Virgil Jackson did quite a job on me," Mathias reminisces. "He got me interested and excited in the decathlon after I thought there was no way I could stay with it. He changed my life, and the decathlon changed my life."

Among the decathlon entrants Bob would meet in the Trials was Irving "Moon" Mondschein, a graduate of New York University. He had dominated American decathlons for years, winning the national championships in 1944, 1946, and 1947. Moon was the strong favorite to be best of the three American representatives at the Games in London.

But Mathias paid no heed to Mondschein or anyone else. Against the very best opposition in the nation, Bob easily captured first place and a spot on the U.S. team. Mondschein and Floyd Simmons also made the decathlon squad, finishing well behind Mathias.

A few days later, the American team sailed to London. This was an older squad of athletes than in the past. Many had hoped to compete in the Olympics in 1940 or 1944. Because of World War II, however, the Games had not been held in those years. The seventeen-year-old from Tulare was a stark contrast to the others in the squad. He was the youngest man ever to wear an American track suit into Olympic competition. He also was one of the youngest of all competitors at the 1948 Games.

London, which had been heavily damaged by German bombardment during World War II, was still rebuilding in 1948. Many Britons were apathetic toward the Olympics; they felt there were many and much more important things than the Games. Still, on the day of the opening ceremonies, with the temperature a melting ninety-three degrees, 83,000 people filled Wembley Stadium. After twelve years without the Olympics, the world was again ready to embrace the international sporting ideal.

Large attendance continued throughout the Games — but good weather did not. For most of the next two weeks, the rain and drizzle were almost constant. Many of the outdoor events became difficult, and sometimes treacherous, for the participants.

The decathlon began on Thursday, August 5. The weather was bad, and there were so many entrants that they had to be divided into two groups. The second group would begin the day's events only after the first group had finished. This meant that the second-group contestants wouldn't complete their events until after dark. Mathias had the misfortune of drawing a spot in the second half of the field. Most of his top rivals landed in the earlier group.

The decathlon is the most exhausting test in Olympic track-and-field. One man is expected to function like an entire track team. The ten events are quite different, and the shifts from one to the other are sudden and jarring. It's as though a baseball player were to come out of a hard game and immediately go out for a bruising game of football.

The ten events are run over two days. On the first day all contestants run the 100-meter dash, long jump, shot put, high jump, and run the 400 meters. On the second day they begin with the 100-meter hurdles, discus, pole vault, javelin. The final event is the 1500-meter run, sometimes called the metric mile.

Scoring in the decathlon is based on the world records in each of the ten events. The closer a competitor comes to the records, the more points he receives. So the athletes compete not only against each other but against the record book.

Bob got off to a good start in the decathlon. He ran 100 meters in 11.2 seconds, his best time ever. Then he ran into bad luck. He long-jumped past the 23-foot mark — his best effort in the event — but in landing he fell backward. The jump was measured to the mark his hand made in the sand — only 21 feet 8¼ inches. In the next event, the shot put, Bob

got off a fine throw of 45 feet. But he stepped out of the throwing circle and was called for a foul. The throw didn't count so he had to settle for a throw of 42 feet 9¼ inches. These two slips cost him many potential points.

Then in the high jump, he came close to disaster. Twice he missed at the first height of 5 feet 9 inches. If he failed on his third try, he would receive no points at all for the event and would lose all chances at a medal.

"That was the moment of truth for me," Mathias remembers. "I needed to clear a height, or else I would have been finished. But I didn't panic. Before I took my third jump at 5-9, I heard a group of fans in the stands yell out, 'Come on, Tulare.' I knew my mother and father and two brothers were in the stands, but I didn't realize that there was a pretty large crowd of other people from my hometown. That was a real thrill. I went and cleared the bar by what seems now like a foot. I think if the bar had been at 6-9, I might have cleared it. I was so determined."

Mathias went on from his successful clearance of 5-9 to soar over the bar at 6-1¼. This equaled the best high jump in the entire decathlon competition, and put Bob back into strong contention. He completed the first day by running the 400 meters in the good time of 51.7 seconds. After five events he was in third place, 49 points behind Enrique Kistenmacher, an Argentine Army officer, and Ignace Heinrich from France. Simmons and Mondschein, the other two Americans, trailed Mathias in fourth and fifth places.

Mathias had become the sensation of the Olympics. More than 75,000 fans came to Wembley Stadium the next day to see if young Bob could beat out the best athletes in the world. They came in spite of the weather — the worst day of a gloomy Olympics, quite possibly the rainiest day in all of Olympic history. A heavy downpour began in the morning and never let up all through the long day.

Mathias was exhausted. He had been so tense after the first day of competition that he couldn't sleep. That second day he ran the 110-meter hurdles at 10:30 in the morning, and was not to run his last event until after 10:00 that night. Between events, he huddled under a blanket to keep warm. For nourishment he had brought along two cold box lunches, but he ate only one. He was just too tired by evening to eat the other.

In the 110-meter hurdles, Bob covered the distance in 15.7 seconds, mediocre for him. Though he clung to third place in the standings, he lost points to both of the front runners.

The discus throw was next. Conditions on the field were getting worse with each passing hour. "It was the worst track meet I've ever seen," he recalls. "If it hadn't been the Olympic Games, they probably would have called the competition off. But you don't call off the Olympics. And the people in the stands sat through it all in the rain. It was amazing."

In the half-light, Bob spun and hurled the discus far into the field. However, before the throw could be measured, a careless official picked up the flag which had marked the longest of Bob's four tries; the officials feverishly searched for an hour and a half before they could locate the tiny hole in the turf where the discus had landed. They awarded Mathias a distance of 144 feet 4 inches. This was the best throw in the competition and propelled Bob into first place. But some who were there still argue that Mathias' throw was longer than the distance he was credited with, and that carelessness on the part of the officials cost him points.

Still, Bob now was in the lead and that inspired him to continue. The pole vault was next, and he had to vault in a ghostly half-light from the stadium lights. The crossbar was an indistinct blur as he charged down the soggy runway with a slippery pole in his hands. He vaulted 11 feet 5¾ inches, higher than any of his competitors.

The gold medal now was within tantalizing reach, but Mathias would need good performances in the javelin and the 1500-meter run, neither of which was a strong event for him. When he ran down the approach lane for his first javelin throw, it was so dark that he missed the takeoff line entirely and his first heave was ruled a foul. He requested that an official keep a flashlight trained on the line so that he would see it on his next approach. With this help, Mathias uncorked a good throw of 165 feet 1 inch.

Sometimes it seems that the decathlon calls for super-human endurance. Asking a man to run 1500 meters — only 120 yards short of a mile — after he has punished himself so severely for nearly two days is almost too much.

Now, at 10:00 in the evening on the second grueling day of competition, Mathias needed to run 1500 meters in less than five and a half minutes to win the gold medal. Specialists in the 1500 meters were already running it in well under four minutes. But for an exhausted athlete on a sloppy track, running that far *at all* would be an accomplishment. He came across the finish in five minutes, eleven seconds — good enough for the gold medal. He had earned a total of 7,139 points, a world decathlon record! France's Heinrich finished second, and Floyd Simmons of the U.S. was third.

As he staggered across the finish line, Bob fell into the arms of his father and mother, who had come out of the stands. "I wouldn't do this again," he told them wearily, "for a million dollars."

Recounting the experience years later, Bob said, "Every-thing was happening so fast to me I didn't have time to realize what was going on. I was scared to death of the whole business. When I finished, I was so exhausted it's impossi-ble to explain. I found out later you always feel that way at the end of a decathlon. But later, when you have recovered your energy, you realize what you've done and the meaning it has in your life. That's when you know it's all worth it."

This youngest of all decathlon champions was born on November 17, 1930, in Tulare, a town of 16,000 people in the San Joaquin Valley of California. He was born only a few months after the Mathias family moved to California from Oklahoma.

Bob came by his athletic talents naturally; his father, Dr. Charles Mathias, had played end for the Oklahoma University football team in the 1920s. The Mathias house in Tulare was within two blocks of two school playgrounds and a gymnasium, and Bob and his two brothers were always playing some kind of ball game or running around the track.

Bob was an accomplished track-and-field athlete at an early age. When he was eleven years old, he was able to long-jump 15 feet and high-jump 5 feet, well above average performances for his age.

Then he got sick. Suddenly he tired easily and didn't seem as strong. It was discovered that he suffered from anemia, a deficiency of red blood cells which results in general body weakness. His doctor-father prescribed lots of rest and large doses of iron pills, and his mother prepared foods that contained large amounts of iron in order to help Bob build up his red corpuscle count.

By the time he reached fourteen, Bob was five feet ten and had a trim athletic body, but he still suffered from anemia. Instead of going out for the athletic teams in Tulare High School, as he had planned to do from early boyhood, he had to confine his extracurricular activity to playing trumpet in the school band. But his condition was only temporary. Within a year, he was well again — well enough to become the greatest all-around athlete of his generation.

Bob returned from the London Olympics a national hero. He was welcomed home by President Harry Truman. He received 200 proposals of marriage from young women all over the country.

That fall he traveled east and attended Kiski Prep School in Saltsburg, Pennsylvania. He played football, ran track, and kept up his training for the decathlon. The next summer he won his second U.S. national decathlon title.

In the fall of 1949 Bob returned to California and enrolled at Stanford University. Football fans looked forward to seeing him carry the ball, but in his freshman year, Bob didn't even go out for the sport. He wanted to concentrate on his studies, hoping some day to enter medical school and follow in his father's footsteps.

Mathias continued to compete in the decathlon, however, and in the summer of 1950, between his freshman and sophomore years, he became the first man ever to win three U.S. national decathlon championships in a row.

The big sport at Stanford was still football, and Bob, in his sophomore year, still avoided it. Then in his junior year he abandoned his plans for medical school and agreed to go out for football. "I just didn't have the aptitude for a career in medicine," he admits. "There was no point in kidding anyone about that, especially myself."

Many people doubted that Bob could make a successful return to a sport he hadn't played in three years. He broke a toe in an early fall scrimmage but plugged doggedly away. He rode the bench most of the early season as the third-string fullback. Stanford, a surprise in the Pacific Coast Conference race, started beating every team in sight. When the two fullbacks ahead of Mathias got injured, he got his chance. His big moment came in a crucial game against the University of Southern California. He returned a kickoff 96 yards for a touchdown that provided the margin in a 27–20 victory.

Completing the regular season with nine victories in ten games, Stanford went to the Rose Bowl on New Year's Day 1952, where the Indians were soundly trounced by Illinois, 40–7. Bob was one of the few Stanford players who acquitted himself well on the field that woeful day. Pro football scouts were beginning to dog his tracks to sound him out about an eventual career in the National Football League. Bob rebuffed them all.

"I played football for the same reason I ran track," Mathias says. "It's also the same reason I entered politics, and why I like it. [He became a California Republican congressman in 1966.] I just love to compete. Just being out there and trying your hardest, that's what it's all about for me. If you win, you're all the more happy. But even if you lose, you're satisfied as long as you gave it your best effort. Professional football never entered my mind, when I was in college or afterward. I played football as a hobby. If it had been anything else, I don't think I would have liked it as much."

Early in 1952, as another Olympic Games neared, the pressure on Bob began to mount. The Games that year were scheduled for Helsinki, Finland, July 19–August 3. Finland would be the smallest nation ever to host the Olympics, and the Finns were preparing to put on an excellent show.

Most Americans would be following the 1952 Games with even more interest than usual. For the Russians were planning to enter a strong team for the first time.

All countries claimed that the Olympics were a means to promote friendship between nations. But in 1952, feelings of competition ran high in the United States and in the Soviet Union. In the States, the Russians were seen as a potential enemy, and it seemed essential that Americans outdo the Russians even in sports. Bob Mathias practically symbolized American ability.

He was now twenty-one and had grown to a full six feet

Throwing the discus

three. He weighed 205 pounds, 15 more than he had weighed in London four years earlier. He was in outstanding form; en route to winning a spot on the American squad, he had won an unprecedented fourth U.S. decathlon title. He was the overwhelming favorite to capture his second Olympic gold medal.

Bob didn't disappoint the track-and-field experts *or* the fans. He won the event by more than 600 points, the largest margin in Olympic history. And he saw that among the athletes, at least, the spirit of cooperation and friendship was more important than political competition. "You'd have to be a pretty hard-nosed hermit to resist the spirit of good-will," he says.

Milt Campbell, a youngster from New Jersey, finished second in the decathlon; and the veteran Floyd Simmons duplicated his 1948 third-place finish with his second straight bronze medal. Campbell would return to the Olympics in 1956 and succeed Mathias as decathlon champion.

With nothing left to prove in athletics, Mathias retired from competition after the 1952 Olympics. But he remained a public figure. After completing work for a bachelor's degree in history, he served two years as an officer in the Marine Corps. Then he became a representative for the Amateur Athletic Union and the U.S. State Department, which dispatched him on five occasions to countries in Europe, Asia, Africa, and South America to organize and encourage youth and sports programs. As one of the greatest Olympic champions of all time, he was treated as a dignitary wherever his travels took him.

Bob married, and continued his travels on behalf of sports. He did public relations and television work and was the official representative of President Dwight Eisenhower at the 1956 Olympic Games in Melbourne, Australia. He even did a brief stint as a movie actor in three films, including *The Bob Mathias Story*. The film is still seen on television. "Too bad about that," Bob chuckles. "It wasn't one of the greatest films Hollywood ever made, you know."

During his time at home, Mathias organized two sports camps, one for boys and one for girls, in the Sierra Nevada Mountains near Tulare. They have become prospering enterprises for the Mathias family through the years.

At the same time, Bob found himself drawn toward politics. He had learned a great deal about world affairs during his travels abroad; and his travels in his own country had kept him in touch with people's concerns. In early 1965 Mathias was approached by a friend, physician Jim Goettle, to run for Congress.

"The Eighteenth District took in my home county of Tulare and all or part of nine other counties. The idea of running for Congress appealed to me. The first thing I did was sit down with professional political people to see how they felt about it. I studied the issues and decided how I felt about the things that concerned the people in the Eighteenth District. I spoke with people and they seemed to like what I had to say about things. Finally, after about six months of thinking about it, I officially declared myself a Republican candidate for the seat."

Wherever he went during his campaign, he was warmly received and large crowds turned out to hear his speeches. Mathias knew that not all those people were interested in his political views. "A lot of people came to see me because I was an Olympic decathlon champion," he concedes. "They wanted to talk sports with me when I was trying to get my points across about the issues."

Mathias is frank about the effects of his sports successes: "Winning an Olympic gold medal helps in business or poli-

From athletics to politics

tics or anything. If people know your name, it has to help —
like an astronaut or a fellow who climbs Mount Everest is
well known. The individual still has to produce, but people
running for political office without a name have to spend a
lot of money and energy to get themselves known. Some
people will vote for any name on the ballot that looks familiar."

Mathias won the seat in the House of Representatives in
1966 by a surprising margin over the Democratic candidate.
In Washington, he soon discovered that it took longer to
master the complexities of the federal government than the
ten events of the decathlon. "I saw that accomplishing things
in Washington takes time," he recalls. "A lot of freshman
congressmen try to set the world on fire their first year. They
aren't successful. You don't make your contacts and find out
who can help overnight."

From his office in the Longworth Building, adjacent to the
Capitol, Mathias worked at being a congressman who would
fairly represent his constituency. In a short while, he developed an expertise in agriculture, a major interest in his
district, and was appointed to the House's Agriculture
Committee. Because of his knowledge of foreign affairs, he
was also appointed to the International Relations Committee. He served well and hard, and his followers rewarded
him by reelecting him to his post in 1968, 1970, and 1972. In
his 1974 quest for a fifth term he was defeated by Democrat
John Krebs. Bob's campaign was hurt by the Watergate scan-
dal even though he was not involved in any way. Also, his
district had been changed to include many voters who tradi-
tionally voted Democrat.

He and his family continued to live near Washington for
three more years. His two younger daughters were in school
— one in high school, the other in George Washington

University. The Mathias's older daughter is a registered nurse.

"We're all very sports-minded," Bob says. "The girls play basketball and swim and play tennis, and my wife plays a lot of tennis too. We're in good shape. And, you know, I have never gotten track-and-field out of my system. Not many people remember this, but in 1955, three years after I won my second gold medal, I took part in the All-Military Championships in the Los Angeles Coliseum and won the decathlon. I was in the marines then, and my performances were way below my best. I was sore for a week afterward, but I couldn't pass up the chance at another decathlon.

"Even today, I find I'm able to do well in the 'natural events' of the decathlon. Things like the 100 meters, the long jump, and the high jump. Events you can just go out and do. Not like the 'style events' where you have to train — the hurdles, the pole vault, the javelin. I recently was fooling around at a high school field and I high-jumped 6-2. I wasn't even wearing a track suit, just a pair of regular pants and a shirt. I surprised myself. It was only a couple inches less than the best I ever jumped in competition."

Bob continues to work for the Olympic Committee as director of the first year-round Olympic training center in Colorado Springs. His sports camps continue to prosper. He talks of getting back into politics. But even if that's not possible, he looks forward to working for the betterment of amateur sports and of the country at large.

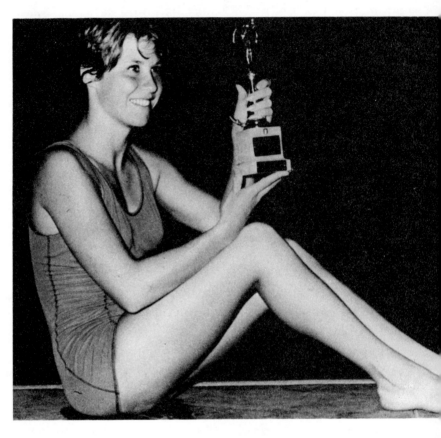

Donna de Varona proudly holds her World Record Trophy in Lima, Peru

Chapter 4

Donna de Varona

When Donna de Varona went to the 1960 Olympic Games in Rome, she was one of the youngest Olympians ever. In 1964, at Tokyo, she capped a seven-year swimming career by winning two gold medals—one in an individual event and another as a member of a winning relay team. Even when she wasn't winning, Donna was one of the most charismatic of U.S. swimmers. Unusually attractive and outgoing, she captured the hearts and attention of people all over the world.

Donna remains one of the most visible—and vocal—people on the sports scene today. As a sports commentator for the American Broadcasting Company, she reports on major international swimming events and conducts interviews with leading sports personalities. In 1968, 1972, and 1976, she was a member of ABC's broadcasting team at the Olympic Games. Donna also serves on the President's Commission on Olympic Sports, a body that has sought in recent years to change the structure of American amateur sports. She is one of the most active and articulate spokespersons for amateur athletes everywhere, and has addressed herself particularly to the special problems often faced by women competitors.

Born on April 26, 1947, she was the second child of David and Martha de Varona of Lafayette, California, a town in the San Francisco Bay Area. With the exception of Donna's mother, all of the de Varonas were athletes.

Her father, an insurance salesman by trade, dedicated much of his life to sports. He was the starting left tackle for the University of California football team of 1937, and was a member of the varsity crew. "He was the first man in the school's history to play in the Rose Bowl and row in the championship crew the same year," Donna recalls. "His rowing experience was very helpful to me later on in swimming. He took the principles of rowing and applied them to swimming—angles, pace, knowing when to increase the stroke, like an oarsman in a crew race would do to pick up speed. He also has been very interested in diet and nutrition all his life."

David de Varona's true love lay in helping youngsters to develop their physical skills. "He would always take time out to help kids in sports," Donna recalls, "sometimes at his own expense. We never had a lot of money. In fact, we sometimes had difficulty paying the rent."

Mr. de Varona has supervised many youth recreational programs over the years, and helped build a gym in Santa Clara, where his family now lives. He also serves as Pacific Coast chairman for the Gymnastics Committee of the Amateur Athletic Union, governing body of the sport in the U.S.

The first of the four de Varona children, David Jr., played varsity football at the University of Oregon. Donna, next in age, was followed by Joanna who concentrated on gymnastics and barely missed the 1968 U.S. Olympic team. The youngest, Kurt, "wants to be the world's best golfer," says Donna. "He's been a junior national champion and has already beaten Tom Watson, one of the top touring pros, in a round. He was worried about being small for a while, but in his junior year of high school he shot up seven inches. He's almost six feet tall now."

As a young girl, Donna showed talent in tumbling. She got her first taste of competitive sports through her brother David, when he took her along to his Little League baseball games. "And," Donna recalls, "the sponsor of the team, Henry J. Kaiser of Kaiser Steel, made me the first 'bat girl' in the local league. I wore a cap with my ponytail sticking out the back, and I really got into the spirit of the games. But I always wondered why I couldn't play. I assumed at first that I would somehow get to play just because I was around all the time, but nothing like that ever happened. And at that time, little girls never came out and asked to play baseball against boys. I'm glad that's changed now."

In 1957, David Jr. suffered an injury that required knee surgery. Following the operation he went to a recreational camp for rehabilitation, and Donna tagged along.

"I was only ten years old," she remembers, "and I tried several different sports. From the moment I got into the swimming pool, I had a great aptitude for it. And I was a winner right away. Only a few months after I started I was swimming some of the best times in the country for my age."

Swimming competitions in the United States are governed by the AAU. In the 1950s the AAU organized age-group swimming programs. Young swimmers, while still in grade school, began competing against other children their age. As they proceeded from one age group to the next, they gained both skill and competitive experience. These programs resulted in U.S. dominance of men's and women's swimming for two decades. Many of the top American champions were swimmers in their teens, brought to maximum competitive readiness through the programs.

Shortly after Donna began swimming, her father recognized her great potential and enrolled her in the YMCA swimming program in Berkeley. "The Y swimming programs around the country really aren't on a par with the programs at the private clubs," Donna points out. "But my parents couldn't afford to send me to a club, and besides, the Berkeley Y had an excellent swimming program. My experience in the pool there meant a great deal to me."

That pool—where Donna achieved her first national prominence—was only 20 yards long. The traditional length for competition is 50 meters (about 51½ yards). Only a few months after she began swimming there, Donna covered two lengths—40 yards—in 25.5 seconds, using the butterfly stroke. This tied her for fifth place in the national rankings of girls ten years old and under.

At the Berkeley Y, Donna came under the coaching of the late Finn Ruuska, a naturalized U.S. citizen from Finland. Her experiences under coach Ruuska left Donna with some sweet memories, and some bitter ones.

"He was an excellent coach," Donna says. "Tough to work for, but a great coach. He gave me tremendous background that I used all through my years in competition.

"To get to the Y I had to take two buses and walk a mile to meet the people who drove me to practice. But it was worth the effort to get there. Later on, though, I had to switch to the Santa Clara Swim Club, coached by George Haines, who later on also coached Mark Spitz. There were several reasons. One of them was the 50-meter pool the Santa Clara swimmers used. But there also was the problem created by the fact that Ruuska's daughter, Sylvia, was his prize swimmer. When I started getting good enough to beat her (she was a

Breaking records

few years older than I was), it was shattering to Finn's ego."

Donna recalls a particularly humiliating time in Detroit in the summer of 1960. "I swam the 400-meter individual medley 15 seconds faster than I ever had before. It was a great improvement and close to the world record. By this time I was training under George Haines. When I got to the hotel room after the meet, I got several calls from Finn Ruuska, who accused me of having taken 'pep pills' to improve my time. He went to the officials with his charges, which were completely untrue, and for a while I was under investigation. Why should I have wanted to foul up my body like that? I was a young girl with years of swimming and life ahead of me. It was a nasty situation."

One could almost understand the reaction of Ruuska and others over the clockings Donna was turning in by 1960. She had demonstrated such proficiency in all the strokes that she had become one of the best medley swimmers in the world. In the early months of 1960, Donna's rigorous training program and natural skills had catapulted her to the top of the 400-meter individual medley world rankings. She was only thirteen years old.

In individual medley swimming, the competitor is required to swim four different strokes during the course of a race, in this order—butterfly, backstroke, breaststroke, and freestyle. In a 400-meter medley, the swimmer swims 100 meters of each stroke. The butterfly, the most tiring of the four, is similar to the breaststroke, except that swimmers must lift their arms out of the water while bringing them forward; in the breaststroke, the swimmers' arms must be in the water at all times. The backstroke, swum on the back, requires a strong windmill motion with the arms and a flutter kick. For the freestyle leg of the race, swimmers almost all use the crawl, the most traditional and the fastest of all strokes.

Donna's skills and accomplishments soon earned her serious consideration for the 1960 Olympic team. And in July
1960, at Indianapolis, she clinched a place on the team as an
alternate. She also broke the world record in the medley
event, covering the 400 meters in 5 minutes 36.5 seconds.
This broke the old mark, held by Sylvia Ruuska, by almost 4
seconds. Unfortunately, the medley was not an Olympic
event in 1960.

The Olympic experience was overwhelming for young
Donna. "Coming to New York for the first time," she remembers, "was amazing for me. My parents couldn't afford
to make the trip. I didn't know what to expect, and everything was so big, so unreal. Everyone else on the team sort of
adopted me. I was the 'baby,' only five feet two [she eventually grew to five feet six], thirteen years old, my hair in
bangs.

"It was pretty difficult for a young girl like me to handle it
all," Donna goes on. "Everybody was laughing at me. I was
wearing my first bra and everyone knew about it.

"We left from New York for Rome. Rome itself was beauti-
ful, but it was extremely hot. Obviously, someone my age
couldn't go as many places as the older athletes did. But the
Olympic Village was fun. I remember Muhammad Ali, or
Cassius Clay as he was then called, running around getting
everyone's autograph, and I remember thinking how big
and impressive most of the athletes looked."

There was also disappointment in store for Donna. She
was on the U.S. team as an alternate and would swim only if
one of the qualifiers was injured or became ill. Donna swam
with the rest of the team in practice—and that was the extent
of her activity in the Rome Games.

"It was frustrating," she says. "It probably would have
been even tougher to take if it weren't for my roommate in
the Olympic Village. Molly Bodkin, one of the country's top

100-meter freestyle swimmers. She too was an alternate, and never got to swim either. But we had some good times together. She was three or four years older than me, but she was awfully nice and we got along great."

If Donna had won a gold medal she would have been the youngest gold medalist ever. The Olympic archives show that the youngest athlete ever to win a gold medal was Marjorie Gestring, who won the springboard diving title at the 1936 Games in Berlin. She was thirteen years and nine months old. Donna would have been only four months past her thirteenth birthday.

Returning home from the Olympics, Donna had little time to fret about her disappointments in Rome. She went back to eighth-grade classes at Stanley Junior High School, and was soon elected president of her class.

She still enjoyed swimming, but even then wasn't certain how long she wanted to remain a competitor. "I was getting interested in other things," she says, "and training was becoming very time-consuming and difficult."

Her parents wanted to move to Santa Clara (about fifty miles away) so that Donna could work out regularly at the Santa Clara Swim Club. Donna insisted that the family stay in Lafayette until her brother David finished high school. After he graduated the following year the de Varonas moved.

Life in Santa Clara, where Donna attended high school, apparently agreed with her and helped her focus her athletic goals. "The world was opening up for me," she remembers, "and I realized how much I wanted to get back to the Olympics and win a gold medal."

The next Games were three years away, scheduled for Tokyo in 1964. The International Olympic Committee announced that the 400-meter individual medley event would be added to the women's swimming program. This was good news for Donna. Once in her career she would break a world record in an individual stroke (the backstroke, in Los Angeles in 1963). But in the individual medley, any record she broke would be her own.

She had set the medley world record for the first time in 1960 at the Olympic Trials. Before she retired, she lowered that record five different times. Her final time of 5:14.9 at the 1964 Olympic Trials stood as the world's best until 1967.

Donna was achieving worldwide recognition in an area other than her swimming. "Donna Dee," as the sports-writers called her, was becoming the most photographed female athlete in the world, as renowned for her physical beauty as for her swimming achievements. In the year before the 1964 Olympics, she appeared on the covers of such notable American magazines as *Life, Time, Saturday Evening Post,* and *Sports Illustrated,* as well as many foreign periodicals.

Donna doesn't recall all this attention with fondness. "People thought it was unusual for a female athlete to be attractive," she says. "We were still fighting that battle then. It got to a point where I was ashamed of my looks. I wanted to play them down.

"That was wrong too, I know. I realized later that there's no reason you should be ashamed of what you are. Instead, you should go on from that point and make the most of what you can with your appearance, your abilities, your intelligence, everything you have going for you.

"When the Swimming Hall of Fame opened up in Fort Lauderdale, Florida, in 1965, I was one of the first inductees and I also was featured as the 'queen' because of my looks. I would never do anything like that again, but I recognize that my appearance helps me in television work because people like to tune in and watch a pretty woman who has a nice body."

It was taken for granted that Donna would win the 400-

meter medley at Tokyo, and she did so with ease. Her winning time of 5:18.7 was not as fast as she had hoped for, however. "I guess it sounds immodest," Donna explains, "but I was so far ahead so early in the race that I eased up in the last half and swam a relatively slow 100-meter freestyle." (Her American teammates Sharon Finneran and Martha Randall finished second and third.)

Donna attempted another individual event at the Tokyo Games—the 100-meter butterfly. She won her first preliminary race, or heat, and finished second in the semifinal. But she placed fifth in the final, which was won by Sharon Stouder of the U.S.

Donna did win a second gold medal at Tokyo. She swam the second leg in the 400-meter freestyle relay and the American team won the event in 4:03.8. (The other members of that winning foursome were Sharon Stouder, Pokey Watson, and Kathy Ellis.)

Of all American women athletes in 1964, in and out of the Olympics, Donna was clearly dominant. Voted the outstanding U.S. woman athlete, she was the highest female finisher in the annual balloting for the Sullivan Award, which is presented annually to the U.S. amateur athlete deemed most outstanding. Men and women compete equally for the award, and in 1964 it was won by another swimmer, Don Schollander, who won two individual gold medals and two other golds in relays.

"Don and I have been close friends since Tokyo," Donna says, "and since then, he and I have worked closely together on promoting reforms in the Olympics and in all amateur sports."

Donna retired from swimming a few months after the Tokyo Olympics. "I swam a few meets in early 1965," she says, "including a big meet in Bremen, Germany. But just before the American indoor championships, I decided to retire. I was only seventeen. To this day I feel I had the potential to go on and set more records and maybe become the greatest woman swimmer in history.

"But I had won gold medals, and with the next Olympics not scheduled until 1968, I couldn't see training another four years. So I decided against training even for one more year.

"I wanted to finish high school and go to college." Donna wanted a career in a profession not normally considered to be open to women. "It seemed to me that any woman who wanted to accomplish something had to have training in law," she says. "Women have been subjected to many unfair laws over the years, laws dealing with property, laws that entitle organizations like banks to treat unmarried women with discrimination by not allowing them loans. I felt if I knew law well I might be able to understand why these injustices existed.

"But after I was at UCLA for a while, I saw I didn't have to be a lawyer to accomplish what I wanted. I thought that getting into media work would be the best and the right thing for me."

Her first television work came in the spring of 1965. She hadn't yet reached her eighteenth birthday when ABC's "Wide World of Sports" hired her to handle expert commentary at the AAU national men's indoor swimming championships. "I was so young I needed a work permit," she smiles, "and they tell me that was the first time a woman ever broadcast a men's swimming meet."

For the next eight years, Donna worked sporadically on special assignments for ABC, handling Olympic coverage and reporting on most of the world's major swimming meets. She earned a degree from UCLA, graduating in 1970.

From the beginning, she wanted to be a spokesperson for

Speaking out for women in sports

the amateur athlete. But she learned from experience that amateur champions in "non-income" sports such as swimming can be forgotten in a hurry. After graduating from college, she found herself at a crossroads in her life.

"I had been bumming around for awhile," she remembers. "I wasn't doing much of anything, and except for occasional free-lance assignments from ABC, I wasn't working very much.

"I had been doing a lot of talking about trying to upgrade the role of women in sports. But to be truthful, I wasn't doing much about it. I wasn't leading a very active life. I was doing a certain amount of traveling—Australia, New Zealand, other exciting places—on assignment or for pleasure. But one day I was lying on the beach at Puerto Vallarta on the west coast of Mexico. I realized I wasn't happy with my life. I felt guilty that other people were fighting for the causes that I should have been fighting for. Just because I was able to get off and take it easy didn't mean the problems were going away. On top of everything else, I also was becoming overweight. I was really wasting time, not doing anything."

Donna decided to return to New York and seek a full-time career in television. After free-lancing for several stations for two years, she landed her contract with ABC. In the next few years she became one of the leaders in the ongoing fight for equality for women on all levels of sports, along with tennis star Billie Jean King and skier Suzy Chaffee.

"Too much attention always has been given to sports for boys and men," she says, "and not nearly enough to sports for women. You know, not all men like sports and not all women hate sports. Those are clichés that have become too widely accepted. I'm a big sports fan. Many women are, and I'd like to see the women who want to participate in sports, either for recreation or as a living, be treated with the same

An active career with ABC

respect by the general public, by the press, by television, and so on, as male athletes. In my work for television I've sometimes been sent to interview a girl or woman who has just done something interesting or unique in a sport. Sometimes that interview never gets on the air. I believe it's because the producer feels that not enough people are interested in a woman doing something in sports. That's an attitude I'm always fighting to change."

Donna's interest in sports for women has taken her to the printed page as well. She has written for such publications as *The New York Times, Viva,* and *WomenSports* (a magazine founded in 1974 by Billie Jean King).

Another of Donna's main interests is keeping physically fit. "I still swim three or four times a week," she says, "and whenever possible, I play tennis or squash. When I swim now, it's for recreation, of course, and I swim freestyle most of the time. But sometimes," she grins, "if I'm in the pool with good young swimmers who are in competition, I'll try a lap or two of butterfly, just to show I can still do it. Obviously, my times are nothing that would excite anybody."

Her career with ABC occupies much of her time. Under her contract arrangement she sometimes works for the network's New York affiliate as a sports reporter for the nightly "Eyewitness News" program, and when the occasion demands it, for the network as a whole.

One of her major interests still lies in her work for the President's Commission for the Olympic Games. "On my own, I've gone to some International Olympic Committee meetings in places like Hungary and Bulgaria to petition members to make changes in some of the antiquated IOC rules," Donna says. "The big change we've managed to have made is to add Rule 26, which allows the federations that govern each sport to make their own definitions of amateurism. The different sports always have handled this question differently, anyway. In skiing, for example, the athletes openly work for companies who manufacture equipment and sponsor their participation in the Winter Games.

"In the United States, the big question we've had to settle has been on the matter of compensation by employers of athletes to those athletes for time lost in training or competing," Donna says. "This never was allowed in the past, but now it's coming about. Corporations should help athletes. The athletes make a positive contribution to the country, really reflect the good of the country. They should be rewarded for this help, not only when they're competing, but after it.

"I'm not advocating that athletes be paid," she emphasizes. "But after an athlete has trained four or five hours a day for several years and gets into the Olympics and wins a medal, he has to make a sudden and major change back into being a regular citizen. Many of the athletes, especially in the so-called non-income sports like swimming and gymnastics, deserve consideration after they're out of their sport. This is done all the time in other countries. But in the United States, we don't help our former athletes, we discard them."

In a typical day for her now, Donna leaves her apartment in the residential area near ABC's New York office, and has lunch with another woman athlete engaged in the fight for females in sports, or with an interview subject.

Before reporting to the station, Donna may have to report to an advertising agency to film one of the many commercials she now does for swimsuits and hair cream. Then comes her stint of several hours at the station, where she helps edit and write the news segments in which she appears interviewing a prominent sports personality. Occasionally, she is called on

With President Ford

First assignment as an anchorwoman for ABC

to do a live report on sports events of the day, including the scores of baseball games or football games.

"When I do sports news," she smiles, "I always try to make sure I know what's going on in the big events for women. I'll give up-to-date reports on a golf or tennis championship involving women because I know there are many women watching the news who'd like to know these things."

She seems very happy with her life today. "I'm involved with my work, my commercials, and my role with the President's Commission on Olympic sports," she says. "It's such a great thing to be involved. I want to remain involved as long as I can. I get to meet athletes all over the world, and it only reminds me of how much I want to do for athletes in the United States. I can't let people have their dreams taken away from them. I had my dream, and I achieved it. Now I want to see it happen for other people."

Go!

Chapter 5

Jesse Owens

In 1976 when the Olympic Organizing Committee in Montreal was selling special Olympic coins to help pay for the Games, it looked around for a spokesperson to advertise the coins in North America. The committee picked Jesse Owens. Owens, a black American who won four gold medals in the 1936 Olympics, is probably the most famous track-and-field star the Games have ever produced. To many people who have no interest in sports at all, Jesse Owens is a familiar name and face. He has traveled around the world, speaking about the values of the Olympics and has fans in all corners of the globe.

This is not to say that Owens has had an easy time. He has many reasons to be bitter about the treatment he has received. For years after his Olympic victories he had to struggle to make a living. Recognition came slowly — and the major reason was the color of his skin.

In recent years Jesse has been criticized and ridiculed by blacks. He is an "Uncle Tom," they say, a man who has accepted second-class status too gently. But Jesse holds fast to his own point of view. Perhaps if his critics knew how far he had come and how much he contributed, they would be far less critical — and much more appreciative.

He was born September 12, 1913, in Oakville, Alabama, the seventh child of Mr. and Mrs. Henry Owens. His father was an impoverished sharecropper who rented his land from a harsh white landlord and earned hardly enough to feed his children. Jesse's grandfather had been a slave.

The child was christened James Cleveland Owens and his parents called him by his initials, J.C. Later on, a schoolteacher misunderstood his name and began calling him Jesse. The name stuck and Owens has used it from then on.

Even before he started school, Jesse had helped his father and three brothers to pick cotton. Henry Owens was fortunate to have four sons to work alongside him. Of the four, Jesse was the least able to help.

"It wasn't because I was too young," Owens recalls. "When I got to be seven years old, I was expected to pick about 100 pounds of cotton a day. I was only four or five when I first started helping. My problem was that I was always getting sick. Every winter I came down with pneumonia. My mother told me that once or twice I came close to not making it through to spring."

In 1920 Jesse's father moved north to Cleveland in search of more and better opportunities. A year later he sent for the rest of the family. "He felt he could do better up there," Jesse said, "and in a sense, he did. He felt better about things, and so did the rest of us. But both he and my mother were illiterate, so what opportunities do you suppose they had?

"Later on, my father, who had a defective left eye, stepped into the street and was hit by a taxi he couldn't see coming. His leg was broken and it didn't heal right. They wouldn't let him work after that. The rest of us had to take up the slack. I pumped gas and delivered groceries for twenty cents an hour."

His early illnesses had left young Jesse a rather frail boy. He was also shy in the family's strange new surroundings in a big northern city. But he had a tremendous desire to make a mark somewhere.

"My father's boss back in Alabama was very resentful when he moved up north," Owens remembers. "My father was a very hard worker, and my three older brothers were too. My father told the man he was moving up north so that his sons could have the things he didn't have. The man screamed back at him, 'Your sons will never amount to anything. Just be grateful if they survive!'

"That white man's words stuck in my craw. 'Your sons will never amount to anything.' I wanted to amount to something. I had to."

Sports weren't a part of Jesse's life during his first few years in Cleveland. His schooling in Alabama had been very poor and he had a lot of catching up to do. He was almost seventeen when he entered Cleveland's East Technical High School. He wasn't very imposing looking and few people bothered to give him a second look.

Charlie Riley, the school's track-and-field coach, saw something in Jesse that others had missed. To Riley, Jesse looked like an athlete. "Besides," the coach said much later on, "he looked so skinny I thought coming out for track would help his health and get him into good physical condition."

Riley persuaded Jesse to take a few tries at running 100 yards against the stopwatch. Several days after his first attempt, Jesse ran 100 yards and when he crossed the finish line the coach was shaking his head.

"I asked him what was the problem," Owens says. "He

said, 'This stopwatch can't be right. It says you ran close to a world record time.' But then he took it to a jeweler and the jeweler convinced him that everything was working properly. That showed me I could become a good track-and-field man."

Jesse, six feet tall and slim and lithe at 163 pounds, became a brilliant sprinter. He ran with fluid grace. Jesse Abramson, the long-time track-and-field correspondent for the *New York Herald Tribune*, wrote, "He is the picture of relaxed ease as he sprints. He never shows any apparent effort. He always appears able to do better."

Owens became unbeatable in the 100-yard dash, in the 220-yard low hurdles (an event that is rarely run today), and in the long jump. The long jump was his best event, but he always preferred running to jumping. While still in high school, he ran 100 yards in 9.4 seconds, which equaled the existing world record. The time wasn't official, because there had been a strong wind at Jesse's back. Still, no high school sprinter, with or without winds, equaled Owens's time for the next thirty years.

When he was a high school senior in the spring of 1933, Jesse also won the Amateur Athletic Union long jump championship. On another occasion that spring he jumped 24 feet 11¼ inches, only 5 inches short of the existing Olympic record.

The following fall Owens entered Ohio State University in Columbus. The university managed to attract him to its campus by offering to find his father a job. Henry Owens was one of millions unemployed during those years. He had been struggling as a laborer. Now he became a messenger in the state office building in Columbus. Jesse worked his way through school by operating an elevator.

Jesse was already twenty years old when he entered Ohio

State. He was married to Ruth, his childhood sweetheart, and was the father of a baby daughter. His job, his family responsibilities, and the burden of school work weighed heavily on Jesse during his freshman year. He trained hard under coach Larry Snyder, but did not have a good year either in the classroom or on the track.

At the very end of the school year, he did manage to finish second in the 100-meter dash at the AAU meet. Probably the best thing that happened to him that year, in an athletic sense at least, was the long jump coaching he received from Larry Snyder.

"He spotted all sorts of flaws in my technique," Owens recalls. "I thought I was doing well enough, but Snyder showed me ways I could improve. He got me to run farther down the runway than I had been before taking my jump. He corrected a hitch I had while I was in the air that cut down on my distance. He got me to refine my jump by practicing doing it over a hurdle."

Early in his second season at Ohio State, Jesse established a world indoor record for the long jump with a 25-foot-3¼-inch jump in New York City. He also was continuing to develop as a sprinter and as a low hurdler, and was running on Ohio State's relay team. He was showing improvement in every event all the time, and his versatility helped him score many points for Ohio State in meets against other colleges.

The best was yet to come. On May 25, 1935, the Big Ten track-and-field championships were held at Ann Arbor, Michigan, home of the University of Michigan. Pitted against top athletes from the biggest universities in the Midwest, Owens had a day that defies belief:

At 3:15 he won the 100-yard dash in 9.4 seconds, tying the world record. He finished 5 yards ahead of his nearest opponent.

Getting in the record book

At 3:25 he took his only long jump attempt of the day and sailed 26 feet 8¼ inches. This broke the world record by 6 inches.

At 3:45 he finished first by 10 yards in the 220-yard dash. His time of 20.3 seconds smashed the world record by three-tenths of a second.

At 4:00 he skimmed over the 220-yard low hurdles in 22.6 seconds to win that event and knock four-tenths of a second off the listed world mark.

Jesse had set three world records and tied another — all within forty-five minutes! It was the greatest performance in the annals of track-and-field. Jesse's exploits appeared on sports pages around the country. For the first time, he was a national celebrity.

The next year, 1936, was an Olympic year. The International Olympic Committee had picked Germany as the host country some years before. Then, in 1933 Adolf Hitler came to power. Germany had been in deep trouble ever since it lost World War I in 1918. Now Hitler played on the Germans' resentments and on their prejudices. The German nation is a chosen nation, he told them, and Germans are members of a "master race." He taught that other races and nations were inferior and suggested that they really didn't deserve to exist. He encouraged Germans to drive all Jews out of the country. And he felt that the Negro race was no match for Germanic people mentally or physically.

Other countries suggested that the Olympics be moved to another country or postponed. But the Olympic Committee decided that the Games should go on as originally planned. Hitler announced his intention to attend the main track-and-field events at the spacious Olympic Stadium so that he might watch his favorite German athletes defeat the inferior people of the world.

Jesse Owens and a number of other black athletes made the U.S. Olympic team. On July 15, 1936, they sailed to Germany aboard the S.S. *Manhattan*. Jesse was one of the best-known passengers on the ship. In fact, two of his three pairs of track shoes were stolen during the voyage by souvenir hunters.

From the start, Hitler made the Games a showcase for his government. He traveled to the Olympic Stadium for the opening ceremonies in a coach followed by a string of black, four-door Mercedes convertibles filled with dignitaries. More than 40,000 storm troopers and other Nazi guards kept the ten-mile parade route clear of traffic. Crowds lined the route twenty to thirty deep.

At the conclusion of the hour-long opening ceremonies, Hitler declared the Games officially open. Competition was scheduled to begin the next day, August 2, and by the time the athletes had filed out of the stadium at the conclusion of the opening ceremonies, every competitor's hopes were stirred to a fever pitch.

Early on the first day of competition a German shot-putter named Hans Wollke broke the Olympic record for the shot put. By afternoon he had won the gold medal, the first ever won by a German in Olympic track-and-field competition. Hitler invited Wollke and the third-place finisher, another German named Gerhard Stock, to his box to receive his personal congratulations.

Later the same afternoon Hitler personally congratulated three Finnish runners who had finished first, second, and third in the 10,000-meter run. Then he sent for Tilly Fleischer and Luise Kruger, two Germans who had placed first and second in the women's javelin throw.

Hitler's personal congratulations to winning athletes broke a long-time Olympic precedent. The Olympics were to be nonpolitical, and heads of state were to be honored guests — not masters of ceremonies. Finally the president of the International Olympic Committee sent a message to Hitler asking him to stop entertaining athletes in his private box. Hitler did stop, and offered no more congratulations in public. There was one problem, however. Neither the press nor the athletes knew what had happened.

Late that same day, Cornelius Johnson, a black high-jumper, won the first U.S. gold medal of the 1936 Games. When Johnson was not summoned for congratulations, American reporters assumed that he had been snubbed intentionally by Hitler.

While all this was going on around him that day, Jesse Owens had other thoughts on his mind. He ran preliminary races (called heats) in the 100-meter dash that day and won both in great time.

Owens's first gold medal of the Olympics came the next day, in the final of the 100-meter dash. Jesse covered the distance in 10.3 seconds, tying the Olympic record. Hitler did not call him to his box and again it was assumed that he was deliberately ignoring the black Americans.

Before he was through, Owens would capture two more gold medals in running events, winning the 200-meter dash in the Olympic record time of 20.8 seconds, and running the first leg of the 400-meter relay team which sprinted to a world and Olympic record clocking of 39.8 seconds.

Jesse also won a fourth gold medal in the event he liked least but in which he held the world record — the long jump. It was the hardest medal for him to win.

During the qualifying round, Jesse had three tries to jump 23-5 in order to reach the finals. This was a distance he had managed while still in high school. But Jesse fouled on each of his first two times down the runway. Another foul and he would be eliminated from the jump competition.

The man who was to give Jesse his stiffest challenge was a handsome blond German named Luz Long. He did not seem to share Hitler's scorn for the non-Germans. Long, who had already qualified, came to Jesse with a suggestion. Jesse had gone past the jumping board on his first tries. "Why don't you pick a spot a few inches in front of the board," Long suggested, "and jump when you reach that spot? You'll still qualify easily and avoid a foul."

Jesse took that advice. He still wasn't in good form, but he managed a leap of 23 feet 5 and $9/16$ inches, barely surpassing the qualifying mark. That afternoon, in the long jump finals, he got his form back and jumped 25 feet or more five different times. Luz Long matched him jump for jump almost to the end. Finally, Jesse won the gold medal with a leap of 26-5¼. Long had to settle for second place.

Jesse's gold medal jump in Berlin represented still another Olympic record, and this one was very special. The record stood for twenty-four years until Ralph Boston of the U.S. broke it in 1960 in Rome. No other Olympic track-and-field record stood for so long.

Luz Long, the German who had befriended Jesse, fought with the German Army in World War II and was killed in action. "Luz and I remained friends for many years after the Games," Owens reminisces. "He was a great competitor who did me a wonderful turn by giving me that advice about my jumping in Berlin."

Jesse remained friendly with other Germans as well. "I've been back to Germany on many occasions," he says. "Fellows that I ran against in the Olympics are still alive. They come to the hotel where I'm staying and we have dinner together. Sometimes they'll bring their grandchildren along. I take great pride in the fact that I'm still very popular in

Jesse Owens on a return trip to Berlin in 1951

Germany and in the rest of Europe too. I find that I get more than four thousand letters a year from European youngsters requesting autographs."

Owens says he never felt slighted when Hitler failed to congratulate him. "I didn't go over to Berlin to shake hands with Hitler, anyway," he says. "What did bother me was the slight I received from my own country. President Franklin Roosevelt never took the time to send me a congratulatory telegram or to send his regards in any other way. That's what hurt."

In fact, Jesse—like Olympic gold-medalist Cassius Clay—discovered when he got home that his gold medals weren't worth much. Faced with a need to make a living for himself and his family, he found the going rough. Finally he became a campaigner for Alf Landon, who was running for president against Roosevelt. Roosevelt won the national election in November 1936 by the greatest landslide in history.

"Poorest race I ever ran," Owens says ruefully. Then he suggests why he campaigned so hard. "They paid me a lot to do it. I won't say how much, but a lot. I guess I was the guy who started the idea of celebrity campaigners.

"You have to understand," he continues, "there wasn't much a black man could do in those days. After they gave me a ticker-tape parade in New York City and another one in my hometown of Cleveland, I had to go out and get a job to take care of myself and my family. The AAU wanted me to run some more races in Europe after the Olympics were over, but I had no money left, none at all. So I came home. They couldn't accept that, and I was suspended. Here I had just won four gold medals, and the AAU, the governing body of amateur athletics in my home country, was suspending me because I wouldn't run a few more races for them!"

Owens was also bitter that he never received the Sullivan Award, which the AAU presents annually to America's top amateur athletes. "In 1935, the year I broke three records and tied another in one day at Ann Arbor, the award went to a golfer named Lawson Little," Jesse remembers. "Then, in 1936, when it didn't seem possible any other athlete had done more to win the Sullivan Award than I had, they gave it to Glenn Morris, who won the decathlon in Berlin. Glenn was a wonderful athlete, but I deserved that award."

Owens doesn't say it, but the most obvious explanation for his failure to win the award, he feels, was that the AAU preferred to give it to a white athlete.

After his work on the Alf Landon campaign, Owens could find no regular employment. He had decided against returning to Ohio State for his senior year. A couple of promised "big deals" fell through. Finally, Jesse took a job as a playground instructor in Cleveland for a salary of $130 a month. Promoters started coming to him offering him money to race against horses or against motorcycles.

"People said it was degrading for an Olympic champion to race against a horse," Owens says. "Sure, it bothered me, but what was I supposed to do? I had four gold medals, but I couldn't eat the gold medals. There was no television then, no endorsements, no advertising, certainly not for a black man, anyway. The only black athlete in the whole country who was a real hero to everyone was Joe Louis, the heavyweight boxing champion. And, of course, he was a professional fighter, making good money in the ring. There was no professional sport I could go into. Baseball and football were closed to blacks, except for the Negro leagues."

For a time, Jesse toured with a circus basketball team called the Indianapolis Clowns. He also played on black baseball teams which gave exhibitions around the country. In each town he would challenge the fastest men to a race, giving them a 10-yard head start in a 100-yard race. He never lost— and he helped attract paying audiences.

In time Owens and his wife and three daughters settled in Chicago, where he became involved in a variety of businesses. Most of them never succeeded in any big way, and a few of them failed. Subsequently, the Owenses moved to Phoenix, Arizona, where they now make their home.

Jesse finally got into public speaking. As a boy, he had been a stutterer, but training under a master teacher at Ohio State cured the ailment. "Now I have probably spent more hours public speaking than I have sleeping," Jesse says. "I've always admired great orators and I'm proud that I've had the chance to speak to the millions of people I've addressed. I hope something of what I've said has helped in some small way."

Jesse has five main speeches in his repertoire and most of his material is inspirational. He is seldom critical of people or of institutions, preferring to promote things he considers worthwhile. Among the things he promotes most is participation in sports.

"We all have dreams," he says. "But in order to make these dreams into reality it takes an awful lot of determination, self-discipline, and effort. Sport teaches those things and others—respect of other people, and how to live with your fellow man."

Owens delivered his most inspiring speech during a return visit to Berlin, the scene of his Olympic triumphs. That was in 1951, only six years after Germany and America had been at war. It was a gray August day, and there were 83,000 people in Olympic Stadium.

"The people in the stands all were cheering for me. They were giving me a tremendous ovation. After I ran," Jesse continues, his voice lifting as he recalls the greatness of the moment, "I addressed them over the loudspeakers. I urged them to stand fast with us in the fight for freedom and democracy under the protection of the Almighty God. I don't know if I've ever had a more stirring moment."

Grace in action

Chapter 6

Tenley Albright

At New England Baptist Hospital in Newton Centre, Massachusetts, the call goes out: "Dr. Albright wanted in surgery." Any one of three people may respond: Dr. Hollis Albright—a white-haired man in his late sixties, who has been on the hospital staff for many years and is also a professor of surgery at Boston University; Dr. Nile Albright—Hollis's son; or Dr. Tenley Albright—Hollis's daughter, the older of his two children.

All three Albrights are general surgeons. And at least two of them are athletes. Nile was once North American speed skating champion. Tenley is one of the great figure skaters in history. She won medals at the 1952 and 1956 Olympics and was world champion twice.

Tenley retired from skating in 1956—and directed her energies toward a new goal and a new way of life. Within seven years she had finished college and medical school, begun to practice as a doctor, married, and given birth to the first of her three children. Through her busy life, well-meaning people have advised her to slow down and not attempt so much. But her many successes are proof that a person can succeed at several goals at the same time and accomplish more than many people think possible.

Tenley Emma Albright was born on July 18, 1935, in the same hospital where she now performs as a surgeon. July 18 has become a milestone date in American figure skating; it's also the birthday of Dick Button, the finest male skater America has produced. He won Olympic gold medals in 1948 and 1952, and was voted the Sullivan Award in 1949 as the outstanding amateur athlete in the U.S.

Early in 1944, when she was eight years old, Tenley went to an ice show. She saw a performance by Gretchen Merrill, a former national figure skating champion, and was fascinated. She promptly asked her parents for ice skates.

The Albrights, totally unfamiliar with skates, bought their daughter a pair with tubular blades—good for ice hockey, but no good at all for figure skating. Tenley's next pair had the proper notched blades and she began taking lessons at the Skating Club of Boston.

Her parents approved of her skating lessons but didn't take them very seriously. It was difficult to get her to her lesson; she had to be driven to and from practice, and there were restrictions on the use of gasoline by civilians because the United States was at war.

Although Tenley's parents did see that she got to her lessons, they wondered why their daughter was so eager. Tenley recalls, "If my mother was supposed to drive me to practice, and it was raining outside, she would say, 'Why don't you stay home today, dear?' "

Years later Tenley realized that her parents, like most others at the time, considered sports a questionable pursuit for a girl. When her brother Nile took up speed skating, he met with almost no resistance. Eventually he became the North American champion.

Like mother, like daughter

Tenley went to private schools, where she was taught that sports should be confined to gym class, "where all we did was skip around in a circle and take a shower," she recalls ruefully. The principal of one school objected to her leaving early one Friday to enter a skating tournament. With her parents' support, Tenley transferred to another school.

In figure skating, even the most talented performer must practice every day for hours on end to become a champion. When Tenley competed, she had to master sixty-seven "school figures." These figures were based on the tracing and retracing of two- and three-lobed figure eights on the ice. Absolute precision was required, and it meant endless hours of repetition in practice. In competition the school figures counted for 60 percent of a skater's total points. Seven judges (nine in international events) watched the skater's every move, examined the figures on the ice, and awarded the points, from a perfect of ten on down. (In the 1970s, school figures are still required, but they count for only 40 percent of the skater's points.)

Tenley preferred the excitement of the free skating part of competition. In freestyle, skaters perform to music of their own choice and can express their own particular flair. Free skating is also far more popular with spectators than are the school figures.

Tenley's coach was Maribel Vinson, a onetime figure skating champion herself. Tenley was only eleven when she first came to Ms. Vinson, but the coach saw her talent at once. She worked Tenley hard on the dull school figures, but she also allowed her time to develop a personalized free skating style.

Then Tenley was stricken with polio, the feared disease that crippled children and young adults. "I'm almost embarrassed to admit that," she says. "Did you ever notice how many athletes my age once had polio? I think that being paralyzed, even for a little while, makes you aware of your

Joy on ice

muscles and you never want to let them go unused again."

Fortunately, Tenley's case was mild and she made a quick and complete recovery. She resumed training under the expert eye of Maribel Vinson, and less than a year later she won her first skating title—for Eastern girls under twelve.

Tenley won the national novice championship when she was thirteen and the national junior title the following year. She was achieving important national and worldwide recognition, and became a member of the U.S. team that went to Europe for several major events in 1951. (She was only fifteen then.)

The Albrights were beginning to be proud of their daughter's success in competition, although they still seemed puzzled at times. "My mother came to competitions because they were important to me," Tenley says. "It was no different than if I were in a school play. Of course, my parents were always conscious of the social aspects of what I was doing," she adds with a smile. "They rationalized my competing by saying I met nice people and got to take trips to Europe."

By the summer of 1951 Tenley was a leading candidate for the U.S. Olympic team. The 1952 Winter Games were to be held in Oslo, Norway, in February. If she were to make the team, she needed to spend more and more time practicing on the ice. Because of her busy school commitments, practicing was a difficult thing to schedule. And finding a *place* to practice was even more difficult. The only available rinks were the Boston Skating Club and the Boston Arena. Most of their time was already sold to hockey teams. Tenley needed a two-hour period during which she could practice each day. Finally she got it—from four to six o'clock in the morning in the Boston Arena.

Tenley remembers many of those early morning practice sessions as an almost spiritual experience. "Skating alone on perfect ice, playing my own music, the sun coming up through the windows. Of course, I forget the mornings when the arena smelled like stale popcorn and sour hot dogs and the rats were scurrying around in the corners."

The long, tiring morning hours paid off. Tenley made the 1952 Olympic team and was a smashing success in Oslo. Though she was only sixteen and one of the youngest competitors at the Winter Games, she finished in second place and won a silver medal. Tenley was the first American woman figure skater since 1924 to finish as high as second. (Jeanette Altwegg of Great Britain won the gold medal.)

Later in 1952 Tenley won her first U.S. senior title. She won it again in 1952, then became the first American woman ever to win the world championship. The international meets were not yet televised. But Tenley's picture appeared in magazines and newsreels, encouraging younger skaters and creating new fans for figure skating.

In the fall of 1953 Tenley entered Radcliffe College in Cambridge, Massachusetts. Radcliffe, a women's college, was affiliated with Harvard University and had very high academic standards. Like the rest of the students, Tenley had to do a lot of studying to keep up. She also continued her figure skating; she would practice from four to six o'clock in the morning, then attend classes, take ballet lessons, and study. By ten at night, she was in bed.

"The busy schedule didn't bother me," she says now. "It probably was the best thing for me. I was very fit, and when you're fit you need less sleep and you're able to think more clearly. Being fit actually gives you more hours in a day, not less."

Early in 1954, a few months after she entered Radcliffe, Tenley returned to Oslo to defend her world championship. Near the end of her free skating routine, she fell while attempting a difficult double-loop jump. Tenley was in first place in the standings when she fell. She would lose valuable judges' points because of the fall, but it still seemed possible she could remain on top.

In the dressing room a few minutes later, Tenley was informed that she had won. Then as she skated happily back into the arena, she heard a voice on the loudspeaker announce the winner—correctly—as Gundi Busch of Germany. Tenley's information had been wrong. She had to settle for second place.

Some of her teachers and friends expected her to give up skating then. "That went all the way back to high school," she remembers. "I had a favorite teacher there who I had told about wanting to be a doctor. He told me not to waste my time on something frivolous like skating when I actually wanted to be a doctor."

But she kept up her skating, and continued to train long hours and take part in the major skating events in the U.S. and around the world. She spent vacations on the ice on Lake Placid, New York, or in Denver, Colorado, both important centers of winter sports. Yet she continued to do well at Radcliffe. She still believes that those who told her to give up were wrong. "The pressure of competing made me a better person," she says.

Early in 1955 Tenley went to the world championships in Vienna, Austria. This time she gave a flawless performance and recaptured the world title. By now the next Olympics were only a year away. "I wanted to get to the Olympics again and win the gold medal," she says. "I liked testing myself, always trying the next step and discovering my potential. I had achieved almost everything possible in figure skating, but the one thing that still remained was the gold medal, and I realized that I wanted it more than anything else at that

Dr. Tenley Albright

time, even if it meant disrupting other things."

She was even willing to disrupt her education. In the fall of 1955 she dropped out of Radcliffe to train full time for the Olympics. "I knew I wanted to be a doctor like my father," she says, "so I knew I'd be back in school as soon as possible to continue preparing for a medical career. If I were eventually going to attend medical school, I knew I couldn't afford bad grades, so I took time off from college."

In the 1956 Winter Games at Cortina, Italy, Tenley was in the best form of her life. This was fortunate because she unexpectedly met strong opposition from an American teenager named Carol Heiss. Tenley gave one of the finest and most exciting freestyle skating demonstrations in Olympic history and just beat Ms. Heiss for the gold medal.

That gold medal performance almost never came about. "About ten days before the figure skating competition," she recalls, "I spiked myself in practice and opened a flesh wound in my left leg. I knew it wouldn't be completely healed by the time the event came up. But I wasn't about to drop out of the Games.

"I had pain all the time I was on the ice during the actual competition, especially when I tried hopping on my toes and doing jumps. There was no way to avoid doing jumps, so I just gritted my teeth and did them. I never told anyone about the injury. My teammates and the coach knew about it, of course. But no one else. The judges couldn't have known. When they awarded me that gold medal, it made the whole thing worthwhile."

That was the beginning of a long tradition for American women skaters. Since 1956, the United States has produced such dazzling Olympic stars as Carol Heiss, the Olympic champion in 1960; Peggy Fleming, the 1968 gold medalist; Janet Lynn, the 1972 silver medalist; and Dorothy Hamill, who won the gold medal in 1976.

Following the Cortina Olympics, Tenley traveled with other top skaters to Garmisch, Germany, for the world championships. The injury she suffered at the Games still bothered her, and she lost.

Then she announced her retirement from competition. "A lot of people assumed I was going to join one of the professional ice shows," she says, "like many of the other Olympic champions have done over the years. But I said, no, I was going to go back home to continue my studies and become a doctor. Nobody believed me. People kept hounding me with offers for a while after I returned home, but I kept refusing. Once they saw that I had gone back to school, they knew I meant what I had said."

Tenley pursued her medical studies with the same drive she previously had demonstrated in figure skating. After graduating from Radcliffe she entered Harvard Medical School, and in 1961 she became a doctor. Then she did further study to qualify as a surgeon.

She feels her skating experiences helped make her a good surgeon. "In sports you learn to keep your mind alert," Tenley points out. "You're tuned to a hundred different things, ready to react. Those are qualities you need when functioning under any stressful situation. The stress of competition prepared me for the stress of performing surgery."

During her years of medical study, Tenley didn't get much physical exercise. "When I was in high school I hated having muscles in my arms," Tenley recalls. "I thought it would be nice when I could stop skating and have 'normal' arms. But being away from skating while I was in medical school caused the muscles to disappear. Then I found it was no fun being unfit. I resolved that as soon as I was able to get back into sports, I would never leave them again."

In 1961 Tenley married Tudor Gardiner, a lawyer. In 1963 her first daughter, Lilla, was born. Elin was born in 1967 and Elee in 1971. "My family is Swedish," Tenley explains, "and those are old-fashioned Swedish names. As for my own name," she laughs, "I think my mother read it in a book."

In 1976 Tenley and her husband were divorced. "Naturally it was a difficult time," she says. "But things don't always turn out the way you or other people would like them to."

Today, Tenley's daughters spend lots of time on the ice. The middle daughter, Elin, shows great potential, and may be a champion someday. Tenley encourages the girls to work hard at whatever they do — and to take risks.

"You have to let children be spontaneous and try things to see what they can do for themselves," she says. "Why take the creativity out of little girls? People tend to box little girls in. They teach them to sit properly and stand quietly and not attract attention. Sports is one place where girls can be free and can enjoy the exhilaration of movement."

Tenley continues to be active in sports, too. She plays tennis with her brother Nile, goes bicycle riding, and skates for fun. She also gives impromptu lessons to local children at a nearby rink.

She gives much of her time to ice exhibitions which raise money for skating and skaters. She has been especially active in supporting the Figure Skating Association Memorial Fund which was established to honor the victims of American skating's great disaster. In 1961 eighteen members of the U.S. national skating team were killed in a tragic air crash. Among those who died was Maribel Vinson, Tenley's old coach.

Tenley is pleased to see that figure skating, always popular in New England, has gained popularity in the rest of the country. "You can thank the improvement in artificial ice surfaces for that," she says. "The kids in warm-weather cities can now skate as much as kids in cold-weather areas."

It's always a busy day

Tenley continues to lead an extremely active life—one that would amaze the well-intentioned people who have told her to slow down. On any given day she may perform delicate gall bladder surgery at eight in the morning, hold office hours until noon, skate in an exhibition in the afternoon, and come home in time to drive one of her daughters to a skating lesson or other activity.

"Many of my friends take part in a lot of activities to get away from their children," she says. "But I want to do things with my children, not get away from them. Luckily for me, they're interested in skating. I don't think I ever consciously pushed them to have this interest, but it's nice that they do. When we go to the rink to skate, we can be together and have fun. Also, we're doing something useful for our bodies' health."

Tenley also continues to study medicine. She attends important conferences and hopes eventually to specialize in heart surgery. "I've helped other doctors perform operations on the heart," she says, "but have never performed one myself. I like the challenge of improving myself in this area." She is also interested in sports medicine—the treatment of injuries and illnesses of athletes.

Tenley also encourages other athletes who are considering a career in medicine. "Many top athletes have come up to me and asked me how much I had to sacrifice to become a doctor," she says. "I say, 'If it's what you want to do, it's not too hard a sacrifice. You find the time and the strength to do it.'"

Along with Dr. Irving Dardik, a heart surgeon from Tenafly, New Jersey, Tenley is seeking to help athletes who hope to become doctors. Dardik was a member of the U.S. Olympic Committee's medical staff at the 1976 Olympics in

Montreal and is one of the most widely respected physicians who treat athletes.

"In just a short time," Tenley says, "we've found two former top athletes who have expressed their interest in the field of medicine and whom we've helped." The two are ex-Olympian Ellie Daniel, who won three medals in swimming at the 1968 Summer Games in Mexico City, and John Misha Petkevich, who took sixth place in men's figure skating at the 1968 Winter Olympics in Grenoble, France.

"There's no reason why an athlete should feel all he or she has in life is sports," says Tenley. "Many great athletes also have good minds which they want to put to use. And a world-class athlete has tremendous motivation and determination, two things every medical student needs too."

The ancient Greeks, who developed the Olympic concept that has come down through the centuries, encouraged the development of "a sound mind in a sound body." Dr. Tenley Albright exemplifies this ideal, and her example has encouraged others—both men and women—to aspire to the ideal as well.

1972 Olympic Trials, Eugene, Oregon

Chapter 7

Vince Matthews

In 1972 American runners placed one-two in the Olympic 400-meter dash. Their names were Vince Matthews and Wayne Collett. On the victory stand after the race, they received their medals. Then — as is the tradition — the national anthem of the winning country was played over the stadium public address system. As "The Star-Spangled Banner" blared out, fans noticed something odd — Matthews and Collett were not standing at attention. Matthews was shifting his weight from one foot to another and looking down at the ground, rubbing his chin with one hand. Collett, too, seemed not to notice what was going on.

U.S. Olympic officials were outraged. Within hours, they disqualified Matthews and Collett from any further amateur competition. The ABC television crews interviewed the two runners in front of millions of American viewers. What were they trying to prove? The answers were puzzling.

The behavior of Matthews and Collett reminded many fans of an incident in the 1968 Olympics, when two other medal winners — John Carlos and Tommie Smith — raised a black-power salute during the national anthem. They, too, were disqualified from further competition. But their action had been planned to make a political statement. Matthews and Collett didn't seem to be political. So the questions about their behavior still went unanswered.

Vince Matthews claims that his behavior on the victory stand was not intended to show disrespect for the United States or for the flag. He does suggest that he was protesting the nationalistic theme of the awards ceremony and of the Games themselves.

"I didn't want it to seem like I was accepting the gold medal for the country," he says. "I don't dislike the country. But I ran the race and won the gold medal for me, and I wanted to show that's how I felt. I was the one who had to climb those fences to train, who had to put in all the time, no one else. I wanted in some way to get that point across."

One thing was certain: The consequences of those few awkward moments on the platform were more far-reaching than Matthews had bargained for. Collett seemed to shrug the whole incident off. But Matthews brooded about it.

"That's all people want to remember," he complains. "All people have to do is say my name, and someone says, 'Oh, yeah, that's the guy who moved around and stroked his chin on the platform.' I wanted my life to come to something more. I wanted the Olympics to mean something more than that."

Matthews's climb to that Olympic platform had not been easy. And his life since then has been bittersweet. He is still trying to make sense of his experiences as an athlete and as a man. His message is, even Olympic glory can be a complicated and puzzling business.

Vincent Edward Matthews was born in New York City, Borough of Queens, on December 16, 1947. His mother was from Raleigh, North Carolina, and his father, who worked as a cutter in New York's teeming garment district, was from Saint Kitts, a tiny island in the West Indies.

Vince's father was an avid reader who particularly loved history. Vince shared his father's interest in books, although it didn't always show in his school work. "I always tried to model myself after my father and grandfather, my mother's father," Matthews says. "They were both good, solid men, even though they never were what you would call successful men."

When Vince was a small boy, he and his family lived in a housing project in Brooklyn, another borough of New York City. But one day his mother bought a ticket in the Irish Sweepstakes and won several thousand dollars. The family bought a small six-room house in South Ozone Park, a nearby section of the city.

South Ozone Park was more peaceful than the housing project in Brooklyn. But life at Shimer Junior High School near the Matthews home was far from peaceful. "It was a tough place," says Vince. "My first days of running came when I'd run home from Shimer to avoid the gang fights and all the other troubles that went on in front of the school."

Vince's parents got him transferred to Junior High School 59 in a better neighborhood. When he was in the ninth grade, a friend of his came home one afternoon with a track uniform and sneakers. Vince was interested right away and asked the track coach at school if he could try out for the team. But it was too late in the year and all the spots on the team had already been filled.

As soon as he entered Andrew Jackson High School the following fall, Vince went out for track. The track coach, Milt Blatt, was one of the finest judges of track-and-field talent in America. He put Vince through some time trials at different distances and saw right away that Matthews had potential for running the quarter mile (the 440-yard run). The Olympic 400-meter run is 3 yards shorter than the 440.

Track suddenly became so important to Vince that he concentrated on running to the exclusion of his classwork. He failed two subjects in his second year there and was declared ineligible to compete for the school. Coach Blatt gave Vince a special training program he could follow while he made up his courses, and Vince stuck with it. "A lot of guys who weren't interested could have forgotten to stay in training," Matthews says. "I found that it was something I enjoyed doing."

Vince regained his eligibility and soon was winning trophies for himself and for the school in top Eastern meets. He was determined to continue with track later on in college.

Upon his graduation in January 1966, he accepted an athletic scholarship to Johnson C. Smith University, a predominantly black school in Charlotte, North Carolina. He had been offered a scholarship at another nearby school, North Carolina College, whose track-and-field program was nationally known. But he was won over by Kenneth Powell, the coach from Johnson C. Smith University.

"I liked his low-key style," Vince recalls. "He couldn't give me as good a scholarship as I could get at North Carolina College, but I liked the idea that Smith was beginning a strong track program and that coach Powell wanted me to be part of his first big team."

At college Vince demonstrated a sharp mind in the classroom and contributed articles and poetry to the school's literary magazine. He was also turning into one of the top 440-yard runners. Coach Powell worked with him to improve his technique and taught him to make use of height. He was six feet one and weighed 170 pounds.

Setting his sights on first place

"I had to work at giving my body a good lean at the start," Vince remembers. "I couldn't afford to be too straight-up at the start because I would lose valuable tenths of seconds. I worked and worked at improving myself and it paid off."

Johnson C. Smith was not the ideal place for an athlete who wanted national publicity. It was small and competed in the National Association of Intercollegiate Athletics (NAIA), rather than in the larger National Collegiate Athletic Association (NCAA).

But Vince couldn't remain hidden forever. The times he posted through the end of 1966 prompted *Track and Field News*, the "bible" of the sport, to name him the eighth best quarter-miler in the U.S.

One opponent proved particularly hard for Vince to beat — Lee Evans, once a holder of the world record in the 440. Matthews and Evans were destined to tangle many times in the coming years.

In April 1967 Vince and the Johnson C. Smith squad went to the Penn Relays, a combination track meet and carnival that has been conducted annually in Philadelphia since 1895. Matthews ran an excellent 440 on Smith's mile-relay team, and also posted a fine 220-yard clocking to lead Smith to an unexpected victory in the 880-yard relay. For his efforts Matthews was voted the outstanding college athlete in the Penn Relays.

Later in 1967 he received his first taste of international competition. He competed for the U.S. in the Pan-American Games, which were held in Winnepeg, Canada. Vince ran the quarter-mile final at Winnipeg in 45.1 seconds, his fastest 440 ever. But it was good only for second place — behind Lee Evans's 44.9.

Matthews finally got some measure of revenge against Evans late in the year. Both were part of an American track

Gaining ground

team sent by the Amateur Athletic Union to compete in several European meets. Once in England and twice in Germany, Vince defeated Evans over 440 yards.

Vince entered the Olympic year of 1968 filled with high hopes. He had worked into the best form of his life and consistently was running times that seemed certain to qualify him as one of the three men who would run the 400-meter event at Mexico City. At the Olympic Trials in Tahoe, California, he reached the final heat. He ran a strong race, but in the last few meters he was passed, not only by Evans, but by Larry James and Ron Freeman as well. The first three finishers would run in the 400-meter race at Mexico City. Matthews made the Olympic team as the fourth man in the 1600-meter relay. "It should have been a happy moment for me — making the team," he recalls. "But I felt I should have made the 400-meter race."

At Mexico City, Vince ran the lead-off leg in the 1600-meter relay. He got the U.S. off to a flying start and Freeman, James, and Evans, in that order, ran the remaining three legs. The American foursome not only won the gold medal but set a world record of 2 minutes 56.1 seconds.

"I was happy to have the gold medal," Matthews says, "and I really thought I was through with track. The Olympic Games wouldn't come again for another four years, and who could be bothered with training four years not knowing for sure it would be worth it in the end?"

Vince was persuaded to try football in the last year at Johnson C. Smith. At six feet one, he was tall enough, even if his 170 pounds was a little on the light side. World-class track athletes who could run and catch a football were then being hotly pursued by pro teams. Several teams told Vince that if he played a season of college ball and showed promise, he would be invited to tryout camp the following summer.

Neck and neck

So he went out for the Smith football team, and made it —
as a third-string pass receiver. Football was a completely new
experience for Matthews. Learning to run a pass pattern with
its stops and starts, ins and outs, was totally different from
running 440 yards straight ahead.

Vince got into two plays, one official, the other unofficial.
With Smith far ahead of Winston-Salem State, he was sent in
for one play. The Smith quarterback lofted the ball toward
Matthews and he caught it for a touchdown. That made the
final score Smith 35, Winston-Salem 0. His other play was
against North Carolina Central. Smith was far behind, and
Matthews went in for the last play of the game. Unfortunately, the final gun sounded to end the game before Smith's
quarterback could throw the ball. That was the end of Vince's
college football career.

At least one pro team was interested in him, however. The
Washington Redskins invited him to their training camp in
Carlisle, Pennsylvania, in the summer of 1970. Vince received his bachelor's degree in history from Smith in January, then spent the next few months running and working
with weights to get ready for the tryout.

The coach of the Redskins was Vince Lombardi, a legendary figure in pro football. Matthews came to camp as a free
agent, a complete outsider who was told he would receive a
contract only if he could land a place on the squad. But
Matthews recalls that all the Redskin coaches treated him
well.

"They gave me every chance to show what I could do," he
says. "It wasn't their job to teach me the game from day one.
But they worked with me to try to bring out whatever ability
I had. I stayed with them for a few weeks. Several players
were cut during the time I was there, and they kept me. But
then they did what I had expected — they cut me. There was

no way I could suddenly pick up all the skills I'd need to play in the National Football League. It was an interesting experience, though."

Back in New York, Matthews entered the Army Reserves to fulfill his military obligation. A few weeks later he was discharged for medical reasons when it was found he had bleeding ulcers. He recovered slowly from the ulcers and began looking for a job. The best he could find was with the shipping department of a department store in Brooklyn. After four years of college and an Olympic gold medal, a job as a shipping clerk was, to say the least, a disappointment.

Then one day, Vince received a phone call from Ed Levy, an AAU track official in New York. Levy asked Vince if he would be interested in getting back into track. There were several meets coming up and Vince would be a good local attraction in his old hometown.

Matthews gave the proposal some consideration. He had been out of training, but he felt bored. He itched to try something challenging, so he agreed to try to run again. First, however, he had to be reaccredited as an amateur by the AAU. His tryout with the Redskins could rule him out as an amateur. But since he had not signed a contract and had received only expenses for his meals during his time at training camp, he was able to regain his amateur status.

"I had no intention of setting my sights on anything in particular," Matthews recalls. "I just wanted to run again. I realized after being away from it, that I liked it better than I had thought I did, and that I missed it. I thought it would be good to run again to stay in shape, and just for recreation. I was putting on some weight at that time and I didn't like the way I looked."

The conditions under which Vince and several of his friends did their running were far from ideal. Since he worked days, he could run only in the evenings and on weekends. The only available field was at Boys High School, a short drive from his apartment. On evenings and weekends the field was locked and surrounded by three high steel fences to protect it against vandals. The outside one was fifteen feet high and the two inner gates each seven feet high. Vince and his friends had to climb over all three before practice, and again when they were finished.

"Thinking back, we all had to be a little crazy," Vince allows. "There were sometimes six or seven of us, and we'd be climbing those fences in the cold and bad weather in the winter, and when it was dark, when we could have fallen and gotten hurt. It was sort of crazy."

Strictly speaking, it was also illegal. The fences were supposed to keep people off the school premises. When it became known that Matthews and other runners were using the athletic field to work out in, the school authorities decided to "look the other way." None of the runners caused any damage to school property and none of the neighbors made any complaint.

"After going over the fences a few times," Vince says, "I realized I was hooked on getting back into competition. I mean, if keeping in shape was all I wanted, I could have found something that didn't require so much trouble."

He took to entering minor local meets. Then as he improved his times, he started looking for bigger meets and better opponents. He was told he needed to join an athletic club before he could get into the big meets. He didn't want to join any of the existing clubs, so he came up with an idea.

He would form his own club of runners. They were all from Brooklyn and they were all thought to be "over the hill" — athletes whose best competitive days were behind them. Vince called his club the "Brooklyn Over the Hill Athletic

Association." He registered the club with the AAU as "Bohaa."

"We all knew the AAU officials wouldn't like the title we had picked out," Vince says. "I mean calling ourselves 'over the hill' and all that. They can be pretty rigid about things like that. So we told them 'Bohaa' was the name of the first Indian tribe to settle in the Bedford-Stuyvesant section of Brooklyn, where Boys High was located."

Vince got himself back into such outstanding shape that as the Olympic year of 1972 approached, he was again rated one of the American quarter-milers who had a chance to qualify for a place on the U.S. team. Lee Evans was still on the scene, competing for a place as well. In the AAU outdoor track-and-field championships early that summer in Seattle, Evans won the 400-meter race — with Matthews second.

The Olympic Trials were scheduled two weeks later in Eugene, Oregon. But Vince had a problem. He couldn't afford to take two weeks off from his job and stay on the West Coast. But if he returned home to New York, he wouldn't have enough money to fly to Eugene in two weeks' time for the Trials. Such problems are common for U.S. amateur athletes. "I was wondering whether all the running had been in vain," he remembers.

A week later, he had almost given up hope. But then a local bank in New York agreed to contribute $700 to send Vince and another neighborhood runner to Oregon and cover some of their expenses. The public never even found out which bank had been so generous; the bank was afraid that hundreds of others might come in looking for contributions to worthy causes. But for Vince, their generosity provided the chance of a lifetime.

At Eugene, the 400 meters was one of the most hotly contested of all the events. The field included Lee Evans, two

UCLA standouts named Wayne Collett and John Smith, Curtis Mills who had held the world record for a time, and Vince Matthews.

Matthews battled through three heats and reached the final field of eight runners. Those finishing in the first three spots would run the 400 meters at the Munich Games. Collett and Smith, the two UCLA runners, finished first and second. This time Vince held on to third place, beating out his old opponent Lee Evans by four feet. Vince had qualified for the big Olympic 400, and this time Evans was to be the alternate and the fourth relay runner.

Some American track officials wanted to reverse the results of the Trials to give Evans a chance to run. Rumors that Vince Matthews might get bumped in favor of Evans were heard even after the team was in Munich. Finally at a big meeting between athletes and officials it was agreed that the results of the Olympic Trials would be upheld. Collet, Smith, and Matthews would run the individual 400 meters.

Matthews sailed through the preliminary heats in the 400. In the first heat he ran an easy 45.94 seconds and finished second. He finished second again in the next heat, in 45.62 seconds. He felt confident and strong. In the semifinal he ran first in 44.94 seconds.

The next day came the final showdown between the eight fastest 400-meter men in the world. Collett and Smith also had qualified for the final, and they were the favorites for the gold medal. Vince was said to have a chance for a bronze medal. But he had different ideas. Crouched in his place, he heard the commands over the public address system, *"Auf die Plätze* (take your marks) . . . . *Fertig* (set)."

When the gun sounded, Vince pounded out of lane four in the middle of the track like a man possessed. So amazing was his start that he found himself far in front by the 200-meter mark. He couldn't believe what was happening, but suddenly he was at the finish line, and no other runner was near him. His time of 44.66 seconds had won him the gold medal.

Only later did he find out that John Smith had suffered a severe muscle pull at the start and had been forced to step off the track. Collett had not run his best race in finishing second. Third place had gone to Julius Sang of Kenya. But none of this mattered to Vince at the time. He was the 400-meter champion of the 1972 Olympic Games.

Then came the award ceremony on the platform. From the moment the "protest" began, it seemed awkward. "The problem was," Vince recalls, "that when Wayne and I realized neither of us was going to face the flag or stand to attention, we just had to wait for the music to stop. It seemed to take forever."

The suspension which the Olympic Committee gave Matthews and Collett didn't affect either of them since they were both planning to retire anyway. Matthews was disillusioned that people paid more attention to his behavior on the victory stand than to his victory in the race.

He came home and drifted for a while. Then he married and moved to Oakland, California. He took a job as a director of recreation for the Tolliver Community Center, where he works with boys and girls between the ages of ten and nineteen.

"I like the work," he says, "and I think it's important work." Yet it doesn't seem to be enough to keep him fully satisfied.

In his spare time Vince began experimenting with a technique of wood carving that he had learned from his father. His work has been shown in galleries and several of his wood sculptures have been sold. Matthews says that his carving is a new discipline, something he can devote himself to, as he devoted himself to track. "That's the kind of person I am," he says. "I need something to pour myself into."

Vince also talks about coaching or teaching and thinks he may return someday to New York City. But he sees sports in a different perspective today. Once the sport was everything, but now it seems to exist only in the past. "There's no news as old as an athlete who's not competing anymore," he says. "That part of me is gone and forgotten.

"Gold medals are nice. The two I won are on a little glass shelf in my house," he continues. "But I don't want them to be the biggest thing in my life. I won a lot of races — but that doesn't add up to a winning life."

Dr. Benjamin Spock

Chapter 8

Benjamin Spock

The life of Benjamin Spock has been full of surprises. As a boy he spoke haltingly and grew to be laughably tall and thin. He was painfully shy. Yet he managed to become a good student and ultimately a widely known and respected pediatrician, a doctor who specializes in treating children.

In middle age he wrote a book about his specialty, child care. Within a few years, he was the author of the best-selling modern book in the English language. Thirty years after it was written, the book is still a standard reference work for millions of parents.

Then, when he was approaching retirement age, Dr. Spock became a political activist. Convinced that the Americans' war in Vietnam was wrong, he joined peace marches, spoke at demonstrations, and even ran for president on a minority party ticket.

One little-known fact about Benjamin Spock — a fact that will surprise even those who have read his books and listened to his speeches — is that he was once an Olympic athlete. In fact, he won a gold medal. This is the story of his career as an athlete and of its effect on his life.

Benjamin Spock was born on May 2, 1903, the oldest of six children to be born to Benjamin Spock, Sr., and Mildred Spock. Ben's father was a railroad executive, and the family lived comfortably in an attractive frame house on Cold Spring Street in New Haven, Connecticut.

Mildred Spock was a stern disciplinarian. As a punishment, she sometimes locked a child in a closet for an entire day. Because she wanted to encourage her children to be rugged, she often made them sleep, winter and summer, in a canvas tent on the roof of the front porch. In summer, she sometimes made the children wear uncomfortably warm woolen clothes.

As the oldest child, Ben Spock may have suffered from his mother's rigid attitudes. Perhaps that is the reason he didn't begin to speak until he was three years old, and only then with painful slowness. As he grew older, his halting manner of speech caused him great embarrassment. Another source of embarrassment was his size. By the time he reached his teens, he was over six feet tall. When he was fifteen, he was six feet four and weighed an astonishingly thin 100 pounds. He must have been an unusual-looking young man, and this served to make him extremely self-conscious. "I was a shy kid who needed constant reassurance," he recalls.

Ben went to the Hamden Hall Country Day School in Hamden, Connecticut, then to Phillips Academy, a prep school in Andover, Massachusetts, more commonly referred to as "Andover."

At Andover, Ben excelled in his classwork. That was nothing new. He had always been an excellent student. Officials at the academy required all young men at the school to take part in sports. Ben had never been an athlete. But at Andover he discovered he had some talent for soccer. Then he became a high-jumper for the track team. His long, thin legs, previously a source of embarrassment, became an advantage in high-jumping. In one dual meet, he went over the bar at 5 feet 6 inches. This gave him a tie for third place and helped Andover to beat its opponent.

After he graduated from Andover, Ben returned to his hometown of New Haven and enrolled at Yale in the fall of 1921. It was a time at Yale when sports and other extracurricular activities were very important. Ben went out for the Yale track team, hopeful that his skill as a high-jumper would ensure his popularity.

"I thought I'd better capitalize on what I've got, even if it isn't much," he recalls.

The young freshman managed to land a spot on the team. But he soon realized that many other members of the team were considerably more talented than he was. In a freshman meet against Harvard that spring, Ben scored one-half point for his team in the high jump. And he won his freshman numeral in track. But he wasn't able to match the 5-6 leap he had made at Andover. He never jumped that high again.

Before spring came, however, he had discovered another sport. On the way to indoor track practice one windy winter afternoon, he happened to stop and watch the varsity crew practicing on the rowing machines in the gymnasium.

"I was standing behind Yale's varsity crew captain, Langhorn Gibson," Dr. Spock recalls. "He was as tall as I was and had a handsome, imperious face — in contrast to me, a chinless, gawky wonder. I was excited to just be standing next to him. Here was an important person!

"He turned slowly around and looked me up and down. Then he asked, 'What sport are you out for?' In a meek voice, I said, 'High-jumping.' If it had been appropriate, I would have added, 'Sir.'

" 'Why don't you go out for a man's sport?' he replied.

Marching for peace, Washington, D.C.

Instead of being insulted, I was delighted. The captain of the crew thinks I should compete for a place! This was a big deal. At that time, crew was the most popular sport at Yale, ahead of football and hockey and swimming. If you were on the crew, you were really something. That same afternoon I went over to the crew office and signed up. The rest of my freshman year, five days a week, I was at crew practice, in addition to continuing with my high-jumping. After that year, I gave up track to compete only in crew."

At the outset, Ben's enthusiasm was his biggest asset in crew. He worked hard at it in his freshman year, but the highest ranking he could achieve was a place on the "M" crew — the thirteenth team and the lowest of all the crews.

In the fall of 1922 Ben Spock entered his sophomore year at Yale. At the same time, a major new face appeared upon the university's rowing scene. He was Ed Leader, the new varsity coach. Although crew had been the proudest of all sports at Yale, it had been a losing sport for some time. Yale had been the most defeated crew in the East, but Leader soon turned it into the most successful.

Ben was still struggling to develop his skills in the sport, and early in the spring of his sophomore year, shortly after the opening of the crew season, he was promoted to the "F" crew — still a long way from the varsity, but a sure sign of improvement.

His height was an advantage in rowing. Ben's long legs were able to generate added speed and power to the stroke of his oar. Looking back over more than a half-century, Dr. Spock remembers another advantage he had as a Yale oarsman.

"I really think it was fortunate for me that I had never rowed before coming to Yale," he says. "At that time college crews were made up mostly of people who had come from the rowing boarding schools — Groton, St. Mark's, St. Paul's, and Choate. And they were all using the English stroke. This depended on a sharp body angle forward and a sharp body angle back.

"On the west coast, at colleges like Washington State and California, coaches began developing an American style, which emphasized use of the legs ahead of the body angles. They found the English style to be terribly wasteful of energy. There's nothing harder than to lean way back, then jerk yourself way forward again.

"Ed Leader came to Yale from the west coast, where he had been helping to develop this new American style. Since I hadn't learned the English style, I adapted more easily to Leader's style than some other people who had been rowing the English way for some time. I had fewer adjustments to make, and this was a big help to me."

Late in his sophomore year, Ben won promotion to the junior varsity, just one step below the varsity. The crew continued to win most of its races.

In the spring of 1924 everything came together. Ben made the varsity crew at No. 7 oar, and quite a crew that was — one of the finest to represent any college of the time. The Eli oarsmen captured several major races and were invited to the Trials for the Olympic Games, along with several other crews.

The Olympic Trials were held on the Schuylkill River in Philadelphia in early June. Yale had an easy time reaching the final round, but so did a crew of naval officers, an "all-star team" of oarsmen who previously had attended the U.S. Naval Academy at Annapolis, Maryland. The final race between the Yale and Navy crews would determine which boat went to Paris for the 1924 Olympics.

Ben Spock recalls that final race vividly. "It was a wildly

exciting race," he notes. "They got the jump on us, and we came down the course a quarter-length behind them. But we caught them and passed them in the last twenty strokes. It was by far the closest and most exciting race I was ever in."

The Yale crew sailed for France on June 21, 1924, aboard the S.S. *Homeric*. The Games were scheduled to begin on July 5, about a week after the men from Yale arrived. The Paris Olympics were the biggest ever held up to that time, with more than 3000 athletes from 44 nations entered.

Among the American entrants at Paris, Johnny Weissmuller was considered the world's fastest swimmer and Charlie Paddock the world's fastest sprinter. The other great favorites were the Yale oarsmen. As it turned out, Weissmuller captured two individual gold medals and Paddock suffered disappointments in both of his races, falling just short of the gold medal each time.

The Yale oarsmen were far from overconfident. Ed Leader wanted nothing less than perfection. "We practiced twice a day on the Seine," Dr. Spock remembers. "The coach also insisted on afternoon naps and a 9:30 curfew at night. And he made sure we were well fed to keep up our strength."

Proper nutrition was a major issue with Leader. When the Yale crew first arrived in Paris, they were shocked by the "continental" breakfast. "Our breakfast the first morning," recalls Spock, "was a shriveled orange—as big around as a half-dollar—a croissant, and a curl of butter."

Leader was not happy with the crew's lodgings in one of eleven concrete barracks the Games' organizers had provided. With the help of funds provided by Yale alumni and other supporters, he was able to rent a large apartment in the attractive suburb of Saint-Germaine-en-Laye. Next door to the apartment house was a renowned restaurant of the period called "Francois Premier" (King Francis I). For the days prior to their first competition, the Yale crew ate and rested very well.

The Yale men showed how fit they were during their first trial heat. The traditional distance in international rowing events is 2000 meters, about a mile and a quarter. The Yale eight covered the 2000-meter course on the Seine in 5 minutes 51 seconds, a record. It was virtually a perfect performance, eight finely tuned oarsmen moving in perfect rhythm with the commands of the coxswain, L. F. Stoddard. Observers of this performance held no doubt they were watching a championship team at work.

The final heat for the gold medal was held at 6:30 the evening of July 17. The Yale shell went to the starting line against crews from Great Britain, Canada, and Italy. A sizable group of Yale fans sat in the grandstands erected on the bank of the river to cheer the crew on as it passed.

There was plenty of reason to cheer almost from the instant the starter sent the crews on their way. The Yale crew was off and stroking at a furious pace. After just 20 strokes, or 30 seconds, Yale already was 15 feet in front of the field. By the 1000-meter mark, halfway through the course, Yale's lead was an amazing 75 feet. The issue was no longer in doubt. As their fans cheered them to the finish line, Yale's oarsmen coasted home a whopping 300 feet in front. Their time was 6 minutes 33.4 seconds.

Rowing is a team sport. But Ben Spock was recognized as a leader of the Yale crew that year. The *Boston Post* reported that Ben was "the best individual performer. In all the races . . . in 1924, Spock passed the stroke down his side of the shell with such smoothness and accuracy that he kept all forward of him in line."

Each of the members of the victorious crew was presented with a gold medal and, of course, each man assured himself of a lasting place in the annals of Yale athletics. "I really succeeded in sports beyond my wildest dreams," Dr. Spock says.

Ben continued to row for Yale in his senior year, and the Eli crew went undefeated. Their most notable success came against arch rival Harvard. Ben Spock left rowing after that, but he didn't leave Yale. He had decided long since that he was going to become a doctor, and he spent his first two years of postgraduate study at the Yale Medical School.

Later he went to New York City and completed his medical studies at Columbia University. During his stay in New York he was introduced to a young woman named Jane Cheney, and they were later married. After completing his studies at Columbia, Ben and his new wife went to Rochester, Minnesota, where he practiced in the world-famous Mayo Clinic. Later he held medical posts at the University of Pittsburgh and at Case-Western Reserve University in Cleveland.

At first Dr. Spock thought he wanted to become a child psychiatrist. But he finally chose pediatrics. "I felt I could contribute more to children in this field than I could have in psychiatry," he explains.

Dr. Spock was carving out a distinguished career in pediatrics in the summer of 1943 when a man named Donald Geddes visited his office. Geddes was an editor with Pocket Books, a pioneer in the publication of paperback books. He asked Dr. Spock if he might be interested in writing a book about child care. "It doesn't have to be very well-written," Geddes said. "It will sell for twenty-five cents, and we think we can sell hundreds of thousands by displaying on racks in drugstores."

Spock had written fairly often for medical journals, but he had never written for a general nonmedical audience. Still, he accepted the proposal with enthusiasm. "I had no doubts I could write a book," he says. "All the Spocks could write. My mother always made us write letters from school twice a week, and she would get angry if the letters were too short. I was accustomed to writing, so I enjoyed doing the book very much."

Because of the demands of his schedule, Dr. Spock was not able to finish the book until late in 1945. Not long afterward, it began to appear in drugstores, supermarkets, and bookstores around the country. It was called *The Common Sense Book of Baby Care* , and it sold at a remarkable rate. The hundreds of thousands Donald Geddes had hoped to sell in time were sold in the first few months. From then on, sales of the book that was soon known as "Dr. Spock" were measured in millions of copies.

The book has had amazing impact on child-raising, particularly in the United States. Studies show that one out of every four children born in America since 1945 has been raised by parents who used the book as a major source of guidance.

Not all of Dr. Spock's readers have approved of his advice. Some believe that his approach to child-rearing is too "permissive." They say that in a Spock household the children control the parents and receive too little discipline.

Dr. Spock thinks that many of his critics have missed the point. "I feel that over the years too many parents have overlooked the basic message which I deliver in the first two sentences of the book," he says. " 'Trust yourself. You know more than you think you know.' No book is ever going to be better than the love and attention a parent can give to a child. Natural instincts mean a lot in the relationship between a parent and a child. People should never forget that."

Then in the 1960s Dr. Spock became a political figure. The doctor had always been a conservative and rather nonpolitical man. But then, during the conflicts of the 1960s, he decided to become an activist. He was outspoken in his attacks on U.S. policies during the Vietnam War and in times of racial conflict. He joined marches for civil rights and peace demonstrations, where he was often doubly visible — because of his tall, long-legged physique and because of his prominence.

In 1971 Dr. Spock became a candidate for the presidency, representing the People's Party, a loosely organized group which saw a need for major changes in government policy. He knew he couldn't possibly be elected, but Dr. Spock used his candidacy to call attention to his strongly held political beliefs. He was on the ballot in ten states and received only 79,000 votes.

In 1976 Dr. Spock appeared as the People's Party's candidate for vice-president. Its presidential candidate was Margaret Wright, a fifty-four-year-old black woman from Los Angeles. "What's the use of bringing up healthy, well-adjusted children," Dr. Spock said, explaining why he had entered politics, "if they're going to die in a senseless war or be frustrated in their adult lives by a maladjusted, malfunctioning society?"

In the 1970s Dr. Spock and his wife Jane were also in the news because of their marital differences. Mrs. Spock maintained that she had contributed a major portion of work and imagination to the Spock book on child care. Yet she had never received any credit for it. Finally, the Spocks separated and were divorced after being married for nearly fifty years.

Despite his domestic problems, the boy who had been shy and slow to speak had come a long way. He had become a

sports champion, a prominent man in his profession, a trusted and fabulously successful author, and a controversial crusader for social and political reform.

His view of sports, some fifty years after being a participant, is somewhat different from the views of men and women who have made sports their lifetime work. Dr. Spock has had very few further dealings with the world of athletics. He never attends rowing events and admits that he pays only scant attention to the Olympic Games.

"It was thrilling at the time," he points out. "But it's rather pathetic to try to keep that kind of glory alive. It was marvelous to be on an Olympic crew and it was marvelous to beat Harvard. But it was four years of hard work. You had to go out the first day of college in the fall and work all year long at it. It was four years of being scolded for making the same mistakes. I enjoyed it at the time, but I was quite ready to leave it once the four years were over."

Dr. Spock never encouraged his own sons to participate in rowing or in any other sport, although one son did become a college oarsman. When asked if sports play a vital role in child development, he answers: "You can't generalize about a thing like that. In some cases, yes; in other cases, no. Sports aren't for everybody, and they shouldn't be portrayed as being for everyone.

"In my case," Dr. Spock goes on, "they were an important part of my life, yes, but only a part. When competing was over, I got out of it and went on to the next thing in my life — to study medicine and become a doctor.

"That's what sports did for me above anything else," he concludes. "They taught me to set goals for myself and then to go out and pursue them."

In stride

Chapter 9

Nell Jackson

Dr. Nell Jackson has her office in the Jenison Fieldhouse at Michigan State University, only a short walk from Spartan Stadium, where the Michigan State football team plays on Saturdays in the fall. Dr. Jackson is the director of women's athletics at the university. She supervises all women's sports teams that play for MSU against other universities.

Dr. Jackson is devoted to competitive sports for women. But she doesn't expect any of her teams to play in Spartan Stadium in front of 60,000 people as the men's football team does. "I would rather see the emphasis on developing ability," she says, "than on the fact that you have to win. I want to see women's athletics grow, but with an educational emphasis."

How does a woman like Nell Jackson become a director of women's athletics? Well, first she is an athlete herself.

Nell Jackson, a black, was born on July 1, 1929, in Tuskegee, Alabama—the home of Tuskegee Institute, which was then a college and vocational training school for black students only. By the time Nell reached grade school, the town was already an important center for athletics, especially women's athletics.

"I competed in basketball, tennis, swimming, and track with the full encouragement of my whole family," Nell recalls. "All the girls I grew up with were interested in sports. I didn't realize until I started going to track meets away from home that some people disapproved of women competing in sports. They thought a girl was masculine if she was athletic. It bothered me for a while, but I was determined to be a successful athlete, so I got over it."

Nell had two brothers, both of whom had the same determination to succeed. Burnett Jr., the oldest of the three, attended Kentucky State University and Meharry Medical College in Nashville, Tennessee. He became a successful dentist in Philadelphia.

Nell was the middle child. In addition to carving out fine records in sports, she began studying coaching techniques at an early age. Later she specialized in physical education for the handicapped. After two years of full-time study and research, she received her doctorate degree in this field from the University of Iowa.

One of the major reasons Nell was interested in the handicapped was Tom, her younger brother. "Tom has been blind all his life," Nell says. "He had excellent training at the University of Illinois, and for several years he was a darkroom technician in the X-ray department of St. Mary's Hospital in Decatur, Illinois. I wanted to study the field of the handicapped so I could learn more about the kind of life Tom was living, and maybe help him where I could."

Dr. Jackson's voice lowers perceptibly as she continues to talk about Tom. "In 1972, for no reason we could see, he was stricken with cerebral atrophy, a weakening of the tissues in the brain. This has left him almost totally handicapped. I

Getting a head start

have him with me now in East Lansing, and I take care of him as much as possible. Here is where my training has paid off to some extent, though I never would have guessed or wanted my brother to end up as one of my lifetime cases."

When Nell was growing up in Tuskegee, things were simpler. Sports were her consuming passion, and she had plenty of company. In her teens, basketball was her favorite game. She went out for the eighth-grade squad at Tuskegee Institute High School. "I was tall and thin," Nell says. "About five feet six and a half—what I am today—and about 115 pounds." She made the second team.

Roumania Peters, the coach of the basketball team, noticed Nell's speed on the basketball court. "She wanted me to come out for the track team, which she also coached," Nell recalls. "So in the ninth grade I did. I was fourteen years old and didn't know much about track at all. But right from the start I liked it."

Nell improved in a big hurry. After just one year of track competition she went with a team of other runners from Tuskegee to the women's national AAU meet in Harrisburg, Pennsylvania, and finished sixth in the 200-meter run. The year was 1944.

"I was a 220-yard and 200-meter specialist," Nell says. "Some girls ran the 100 or long-jumped, in addition to running the 200. But I stayed with the 200 meters, or 220 yards, which is a few feet longer. There weren't really all that many choices at that time. The 220 was the longest event a woman could run then. There were a lot of so-called 'studies' around then showing how 'dangerous' it was for women to run longer distances, that they would upset their chemical and physical makeup. It didn't make a great deal of sense to me, but there was nothing I could do about it. So I ran the 220."

Tuskegee Institute was a hotbed of women's track. There

Breaking the tape

1948 U.S. Women's Olympic Track-and-Field Team—Nell Jackson is in the second row, extreme right

were so many topflight girls competing at both the high school and college that a separate amateur club was formed to incorporate the best of the girls for national events. It was called the Tuskegee Institute Track-and-Field Club. In 1945 a group of Tuskegee high school and college girls went to the indoor AAU nationals and ran off with the 440-yard relay championship. As a sixteen-year-old, Nell was the youngest of the four relay runners, but she ran the lead-off leg in fine style, bringing her three teammates a lead they never gave up.

The young women from Tuskegee continued to prosper on the national scene. In 1947 a foursome from the Institute won the outdoor AAU 400-meter relay title. They were to win the same title five years in a row. Nell ran the fourth, or anchor leg, for the victors in 1947, 1948, and 1951, and ran the opening leg in 1949 and 1950. The Tuskegee victory in 1951 was recorded in 49.8 seconds, the fastest clocking posted to that time in the national AAU meet.

In 1948 the Olympic Games were scheduled to resume after a twelve-year hiatus. (The 1940 and 1944 Games had been canceled because World War II occupied most of the countries of the world.) In Tuskegee interest in women's track reached fever pitch. The city boasted several of the world's best female athletes, and it seemed certain that the town would be well represented when the Games began in London. In the months leading up to the Games, the women from Tuskegee were in top form. In the national AAU meet at Grand Rapids, Michigan, in the first week of July, they won the team title by a 36-point margin. In the individual 200-meter race, Nell placed third, putting her in a prominent spot as the Trials neared.

The Olympic Trials were held the following week in Providence, Rhode Island. Nell won a spot on the U.S. squad by placing second to Audrey Patterson of Nashville in the 200-meter run. She was one of eleven women track-and-field competitors from the U.S. With the full Olympic team of several hundred, Nell sailed for London in late July. "It was the first time I ever traveled by boat," she recalls, "and it was quite an experience."

To compete in the Olympic Games is the dream of many amateur athletes. Vying with athletes from other lands represents the zenith of amateur sport; victory is just an added bonus. Nell didn't win any medals at the 1948 Olympics. In the first-round heat of the 200-meter event, she placed third, inches behind Shirley Strickland of Australia. Both runners were clocked at 25.8 seconds, but only one could go on to the semifinals. Nell was eliminated.

The same fate befell the Tuskegee 400-meter relay team. In the first heat they placed third, just two-tenths of a second behind the runners-up. Only two teams qualified, so again Tuskegee was shut out.

Tuskegee had lots to be proud of, however. Only one U.S. woman captured a gold medal in track-and-field in London—Alice Coachman, who won the long jump. A few years earlier Alice had been a member of a title-winning relay team at Tuskegee before moving to Albany State College in Georgia. At least, the town of Tuskegee could claim credit for having sent Alice on her way to Olympic glory.

The women's track-and-field competition at the 1948 Games was dominated by Fanny Blankers-Koen, a Dutch mother of four. In one of the most amazing performances ever given by a woman in an Olympics, Fanny captured four gold medals. She won the 100-meter and 200-meter dashes, and the 80-meter hurdles, and she ran for the Netherlands' first-place 400-meter relay team. Her flashing feet earned her the nickname, "The Flying Housewife."

Welcome home!

"I was disappointed that I didn't do better in my races," recalls Nell, "especially the 200-meter individual race. I thought I would at least make it to the finals where, with a break or two, anyone can get a good jump and win the gold. But I would have to say that, medal or no medal, the Olympics were one of the greatest experiences of my life. It's something I never would have traded for anything else."

Nell had the misfortune of reaching her peak competitive years between Olympiads. In 1948 she hadn't been quite ready to defeat the best in the world. By the 1952 Games in Helsinki, Finland, she was nearing the end of her competitive career, and her records were being surpassed by younger runners.

Nonetheless, at her athletic height, Jackson dominated her event. In the years 1949 and 1950 she was perhaps the best female 200-meter sprinter in the world. In 1949 she won the national 200-meter title in 24.2 seconds, clipping two-tenths of a second off the American record which had stood for fourteen years. In 1950 Nell successfully defended her national title in 25 seconds flat.

Still in top form, she was chosen for the U.S. squad at the first Pan-American Games ever held. This Olympic-like competition was held in the summer of 1951 in Buenos Aires, Argentina, for athletes from North and South American countries.

In Buenos Aires, Nell finished second in the 200 meters behind American teammate Mae Faggs, and helped the 400-meter team win the gold medal in the relay event. The gold medal she received for her share in that victory is one of her prized possessions to this day. "It wasn't an Olympic medal," she says, "but it still gave me great satisfaction."

By this time, Nell had graduated from Tuskegee Institute. She went to Wellesley College in Massachusetts for one year, then transferred to Springfield College in Massachusetts, one of America's leading schools for physical education. There she earned a master's degree in the summer of 1953.

Nell then was invited to return home to become an instructor in the physical education department of Tuskegee Institute. Shortly after she took the job, Cleve Abbott, who had been women's track-and-field coach at the college for many years, died suddenly. Nell was named to succeed him.

"I had always wanted a career in coaching," she says, "and coaching the girls at Tuskegee gave me my first opportunity to show what I could do."

Even though she wasn't much older than some of her students, Nell did so well that only three years later she was asked to direct the women's track team at the Melbourne Olympics. She was twenty-seven and was one of the youngest head coaches of any sport in Olympic history.

At Melbourne, the American women won one gold medal. That one was captured by Mildred McDaniel in the high jump with a world record leap of 5 feet 9¼ inches. Nell derived great satisfaction from Mildred's victory. "She was one of the members of my team at Tuskegee," she points out. "We lost out in some other events where I thought we had a chance at medals, but it certainly was gratifying to see someone I had been working with at Tuskegee take a gold."

In 1960, after eight years at Tuskegee, Nell went back to school. She enrolled as a doctoral candidate at the University of Iowa, specializing in physical education of the handicapped. After she received her degree, she rejoined the Tuskegee faculty as an assistant professor in the physical education department.

At the end of another two years at Tuskegee, Dr. Jackson returned to the Midwest. First she taught at Illinois State University at Normal, Illinois. Then she went to the University of Illinois at Champaign, where she taught undergraduate and graduate courses. She also organized and coached the Illinois Track Club for Girls, the first women's track-and-field team at the university. She wrote prolifically, publishing many magazine articles and one book, *Track and Field for Girls and Women*, which has been praised as one of the most definitive works on the subject.

In 1968 Nell Jackson became chairperson of the U.S. Women's Track-and-Field Committee, chairperson of the AAU Women's Track-and-Field Committee, and a member of the Board of Directors of the U.S. Olympic Committee. Then in 1972 she coached the women's track-and-field squad at the Munich Olympics. Women's track-and-field was better organized and far more advanced in Europe — particularly in the Soviet Union and East Germany. Nell's American team won no gold medals, but the 1600-meter relay foursome of Mable Fergerson, Madeline Manning, Cheryl Toussaint, and Kathy Hammond won a silver medal, and Kathy Hammond in the 400-meter run and Kathy Schmidt in the javelin won bronzes.

In the summer of 1973 Nell was offered a new challenge — the job as director of women's athletics at Michigan State. She accepted and began work that fall.

"I saw it as a tremendous challenge," Nell says. "The university had begun a women's athletics program the year before I came. Before that, women's sports had been directed by the women's physical education department. This was true at most other schools as well. But by hiring me and asking me to direct a full-scale program for women's competitive athletics, Michigan State showed it was interested in allowing as many women to compete as wanted to. This was also my objective. I felt I could accomplish something here."

Before Dr. Jackson came to Michigan State, the university's

Dr. Nell Jackson, director of women's athletics, Michigan State University

entire budget for women's sports was $34,000. Within her first six months, she managed to get the school to raise that figure to $84,000. Two years later the school spent more than $160,000 on its women's sports program—still a small amount compared to the huge sums universities spend on men's athletics.

"The difference is that women's sports is not a highly pressured environment," Dr. Jackson says. "People here at MSU cooperate and are willing to help. This is what the women's program needs. We're on the right road. But as the program continues to develop, here and at other universities, there will be a need for more money and public recognition. Women have never said they want equal money to men for sports programs, but they do want to have a situation that isn't totally unfair, the way it was for so many years."

Nell, who has never married, is a quiet, soft-spoken woman. Her work is her driving force in life. Through her efforts, women's sports at Michigan State are becoming a recognized and honored part of the athletic program. Her office in the Jenison Fieldhouse is a symbol of the changes she is helping to make.

"Varsity teams should have offices outside the physical education department," she says. "They're really quite different entities, and they need room of their own."

Physical education courses are available to all students at the university and are important. But Nell Jackson is particularly interested in women who want to come out and be on a team that competes regularly with other teams.

Many people have commented that Nell is the first black woman to become athletic director at a large university. Nell is proud of having reached her present position, but she does not feel that race is much of an issue.

"I don't believe anyone favored me or held me back from reaching my goals because I'm black," she says. "I think the people who hired me thought I was the best qualified for the job. I've never had a single problem with any young women athletes I've coached that had anything to do with race."

Her main interest lies in working against the restrictions placed on women in competitive sports. She has seen big changes in her career, but there is still much more to do. She is active in several of the groups that govern women's athletics and supports their efforts to increase opportunities for athletic competitions between women in schools, colleges, and universities.

She is especially encouraged by the number of women who are entering coaching. Along with her other duties at Michigan State, she advises prospective women coaches who are doing graduate work in physical education.

"There has always been a certain number of women going into the teaching of physical education," she says. "But coaches have been harder to find. For many years, women's and girls' teams have been coached by men. But now the young women who participate on one level or another are returning and giving something back to sports.

"It's one of the healthiest indications of all that women's sports are on the verge of their biggest explosion yet," Dr. Jackson concludes.

Bill Bradley with the New York Knicks

Chapter 10

Bill Bradley

When Bill Bradley was at Princeton University, he was an honor student in political science. Most people who knew him assumed that when he graduated he would become a lawyer or a public servant. One day he might well hold a high office in government.

Bill was also a basketball player — not an ordinary player, but a great one. He broke many scoring records at Princeton and made an ordinarily undistinguished team into a national power. While still at Princeton he was chosen to the 1964 U.S. Olympic team and became one of its stars. The next season, in his senior year, he carried his team to the semifinals of the NCAA tournament.

Still, he didn't seem the type to become a professional. His friends were confident that he would leave his basketball days behind when he graduated. "People were so sure I was going to run for office, or practice law, or enter business, that they nearly had me convinced that basketball was not a good way of life," he says. "But I had a great love for the game and the longer I played, the more I loved it.

"During the years my attitudes changed as I had a chance

169

to mature and learn different things about myself," Bradley continues. "One of the things I discovered about myself and basketball was that I was not just a ballplayer, but that basketball was work that I enjoyed."

Bradley's decision to stay in basketball—for some eleven years after graduating Princeton—was all the more interesting when one realizes that he was never the star in the professional game that he had been in college. He earned more than $300,000 a year, but was overshadowed by Willis Reed, Walt Frazier, and other Knick stars. He found that he was almost too slow for professional ball and that his shooting talent, so impressive in college, was not very remarkable in the pros. He gained his place on the Knicks, not by scoring or flashy dribbling, but by becoming a team player and by playing smart team basketball.

Bill Bradley was born on July 28, 1943, in Crystal City, Missouri, on the banks of the Mississippi River, about forty miles from St. Louis. His father (now retired) was president of a bank. Bill says his father is the person he admired most during his growing-up years. "My father is a good man," he says. "To him, life is finding your own virtues and strengths and developing them."

Bill describes his mother as "an energetic mother who spent a lot of time at church. Where my father insisted on manners, my mother insisted on success. I took lessons in practically everything: dancing, trumpet, French horn, piano, boxing, tennis, golf, swimming, canoeing, typing, French, and horseback-riding. By the time I was fourteen, I had become self-motivated."

The Bradley family shuttled back and forth between Crystal City and their vacation home in West Palm Beach, Florida. When he arrived in Missouri or Florida after a long absence,

Bill found that the basketball court was a good place to meet friends. His father had built an asphalt court in the backyard of their home in Crystal City when Bill was nine. Soon after, the boy began playing regularly at a local YMCA. As a teenager, he attended a summer basketball camp in St. Louis conducted by "Easy" Ed Macauley, then a prominent professional player.

"I enjoyed playing very much," Bill recalls, "and I wanted to work at improving myself all the time. But I missed one thing after I took up basketball seriously. When I was a young boy, my grandfather and I used to take leisurely walks along the banks of the Mississippi, and he would tell stories about his early life in Germany. I guess he never knew how much I enjoyed those stories, but I developed other interests and he got older, and the walks stopped."

By the time young Bradley entered Crystal City High School, he was six feet three. His height was one natural gift he enjoyed as an athlete. And he seemed to have a touch for shooting a basketball—a skill he developed during long hours of practice.

Bill is the first person to admit that he doesn't have great physical gifts. "I'm not fast and I don't jump well," he says. "About the fastest I ever ran for 100 yards was 11.2 seconds, and I did that as a high school freshman, when most young athletes are fastest. I don't jump well and I couldn't lift a barbell without a derrick. I tried eating a lot of that breakfast food, 'The Breakfast of Champions,' " he adds with a smile, "but I never could get to look anything like the guy on the cereal box."

Bradley improved his jumping by practicing with weights in his shoes. He improved his agility by lining up chairs in an empty school basement and dribbling around them. To improve his coordination and dribbling skill even further, he devised some eyeglass frames whose bottom half was covered with cardboard to prevent him from looking at the ball when he was dribbling. But his chief asset as a basketball player was his shooting. This talent helped earn him recognition as a high school All-America in his senior year. By this time Bill had grown to his full six feet five.

In their senior year, great high school athletes suddenly become very popular among college recruiters. Head coaches and their assistants arrive for personal visits, waving offers of athletic scholarships and boasting about the virtues of their schools. College recruiting of athletes has often been criticized. The fact is, colleges can gain both money and prestige if they have championship football or basketball teams. They fill their stadiums and field houses with paying customers, collect money from television for the right to broadcast games, and receive large gifts from former students who are proud of their school's athletic success.

The pressure on college coaches to build winning teams is intense. In basketball there is often one assistant coach whose main job is to recruit. He travels around the country, visits outstanding high school athletes, and tries to sell them on attending the college he represents.

Students on a college athletic scholarship can legally receive room, board, and tuition. In addition, they can receive a small amount for books, laundry, and other normal expenses. Many athletes have received much more — cash payments, "loans" that need never be repaid, cars, and expensive clothes.

The rush for Bill Bradley lasted most of his senior season in high school. Adolph Rupp, the famous coach at the University of Kentucky, paid a surprise visit to the office of Bill's father. Dozens of other schools sent representatives.

Bill had two great advantages over many other athletes.

Putting Princeton on the basketball map

First, his family was well-to-do, so he knew he would be going to college in any case. Second, he was a brilliant student. Any university would be proud to have him even if he never touched a basketball. Bill was interested in schools with strong academic departments; their basketball program was only one of many considerations. He narrowed his choice to either Duke University in Durham, North Carolina, or Princeton University in New Jersey. He finally chose Princeton.

Even before he had played his first varsity game at Princeton, Bill gained wide attention on the sports pages. Playing for the freshman team in 1961–62, he connected on fifty-seven consecutive free throws, breaking an NCAA varsity record. Because Bill was not playing for the varsity, however, the record didn't count.

Bill joined the Princeton Tigers for the 1962–63 campaign, and began rewriting the university's basketball record book. He averaged 27.3 points per game as a sophomore and made a sensational 89.3 percent of his shots from the foul line. The next year he was even more outstanding. He increased his scoring average to 32.3 points per game and led the nation's collegiate players in total field goals, total free throws, and total points.

From his first game as a sophomore, he was thought to be the finest player ever to appear in the Ivy League. But the Ivy League, made up of distinguished Eastern universities (Harvard, Yale, Columbia, Dartmouth, and others), was hardly a big-time league for basketball. The schools in the league had agreed in the 1950s to de-emphasize athletics and to give up trying to match the giant public universities in football and basketball. Sports fans and writers recognized Bradley as a great player, but he was playing in a minor league. After his junior year, Bill was named to most All-

America teams as one of the top five college players in the country. This was a rare distinction for an Ivy Leaguer. He also got the chance to prove his talents to the country and the world. He was chosen as one of the twelve players for the American team that would compete in the Olympic Games at Tokyo. At twenty-one, he was the youngest player selected to the squad, and the only player who still hadn't completed his college basketball career.

The Olympics were to be held October 10–24, 1964. Bill went into pre-Olympic training in September and didn't get to class until the last days of October.

"I missed the first six weeks," he said. "To keep up, I had to take several books with me to Tokyo, so I wouldn't be far behind when I got back to school."

The Olympic basketball competition that year was not overly strenuous for the American team. The U.S. had never lost an Olympic basketball game and was not expected to lose the one in 1964. Bradley recalls that some countries were improving, but they still had a long way to go. "Truthfully," he says, "none of us ever felt at any time we were in danger of losing to any of the other teams in the tournament.

"The team's only close call came against Yugoslavia. With two minutes to go in our game against the Yugoslavs, we had only a 2-point lead," Bill remembers. "I was on the bench at the time, and Hank Iba, our coach, sent me back in and told me to try to do something about the score — in other words, shoot. I made three shots in a row and we finally won by 8 points, 69–61."

Bradley recalls the Olympics as his greatest experience in amateur basketball, "bigger than anything I did in college, even though we fully expected to win the gold medal."

Bill is also concerned about the future of the Olympic

Games: "Many people have called for the abolition of the Olympics, claiming that they have become too expensive, too political, and too dangerous. I believe that the Olympics should be continued, but only with drastic modification."

The most surprising of Bradley's suggestions for change is his proposal that team sports, such as basketball, be eliminated from the Games. "Each team sport should have a separate world tournament," he says. "It would reduce the number of athletes physically present at the Games, and it would allow several places in the world to share the prestige of being host to a world championship tournament.

"Besides," he continues, "team sports emphasize nationalism, and the thrust of a purified Olympics should be away from nationalism. The individual should be the central figure."

Bradley also feels that the Olympics should be open to everyone, amateur and professional alike. "The only eligibility requirement should be a person's skill, not whether he's considered a pro or an amateur," Bradley says. "Amateurism is impossible to interpret and there is no uniformity among nations as to what even constitutes amateurism. At the Tokyo Olympics, we beat the Russians in the finals. Two years later I played for a pro team from Milan, Italy, and I played against the Russian Army club in the semifinals of the European Cup. Man for man, the Russian starting five was the same as the Olympic team's starting five in 1964. The army pays them to play basketball, but by Olympic standards they were amateurs.

"And," Bill goes on, "while the Olympics celebrate the fastest, the strongest, and the most agile among us, why not also recognize creativity, spirituality, and tolerance? A film festival, poetry readings, concerts, cultural shows could run simultaneously with the athletic events. The whole person might be the theme of the Games. I believe this is what the Olympics should be."

During Bradley's last year at Princeton, the basketball schedule was upgraded to include some nationally rated teams and to give Bill a better showcase for his talents. He showed the same devastating scoring abilities against the highest caliber competition that he had previously shown when Princeton was facing primarily Eastern rivals. In fact, surrounded by a capable supporting cast, Bradley led the Tigers to the semifinals of the postseason NCAA tournament.

Bradley averaged 30.2 points per game in his senior year. He closed out three years of collegiate play with 2503 points, the third highest total ever recorded up to that time. His greatest game as a collegian was probably against the University of Michigan — the team ranked first in the U.S. — in Madison Square Garden. Michigan was expected to trounce the Tigers. But with less than five minutes remaining, Princeton was ahead 75–63, thanks mostly to Bill Bradley. Then Bill fouled out of the game. In the next few minutes, Princeton fell apart. Michigan scored 17 points in a row and won 80–75. Before fouling out, Bill had scored 41 of his team's points — more than half.

In the semifinals of the NCAA tournament, Princeton and Michigan met again. This time, the game was not even close, Michigan winning by 17 points, 93–76. In the consolation game for third place in the tournament, Princeton played Wichita State. Though he concentrated, as always, on passing as much as shooting, Bill had scored 32 points — more than his usual average for an entire game — by the end of the first half.

Bill van Breda Kolff, the Princeton coach, instructed Bill's teammates to keep passing the ball to him in the second half. Perhaps in his last college game Bradley could set a one-game tournament scoring record. "I thought it was odd they kept giving the ball back to me," recalls Bradley. "I thought they wanted to make sure of some sort of record for Princeton. Finally I agreed that I would keep shooting until I missed."

Bill proceeded to sink 16 consecutive points in a five-minute span and finally wound up with 58 points, 2 better than the previous record. Princeton won the game 118–82. Though UCLA beat Michigan in the finals and won the championship, Bradley was named the outstanding player in the tournament.

Praise came in from around the country. Bill was named to every All-America squad and was in demand for publicity appearances. But he had disappeared. Where was he? In the home of a friend working on his senior paper. "The thesis was 150 pages long and dealt with 'The 1940 U.S. Senatorial Campaign in Missouri.' The winner of that election was Harry S. Truman, who became president in 1945." Truman was one of Bill's earliest heroes.

Bill graduated from Princeton in the summer of 1965 with an A average and honors in his major subject, history. Then it was time for him to make a big decision. The New York Knicks, then one of the worst teams in the NBA, drafted him and were willing to pay him a handsome salary to play for them in 1965–66. But Bill had a rare opportunity. He had been selected as a Rhodes Scholar, a great honor that recognized his abilities both as a student and as an athlete. The scholarship entitled him to two years of postgraduate study at Oxford University in England. The problem was that he couldn't accept the scholarship and play for the Knicks at the same time. Finally he took the scholarship and went to England to study philosophy, economics, and politics.

He couldn't stay completely away from basketball, so he joined the Simmenthal team of Milan in the Italian League and commuted between England and Italy to compete for the Simmenthal club. "The competition wasn't especially strong," Bill recalls, "but it was a great chance to play basketball. I don't think the two years I spent at Oxford would have meant as much to me as they did if I hadn't also been able to take part in basketball."

Bradley left a considerable imprint on the court scene in Europe. Whenever the Simmenthal team played, it attracted sizable crowds who turned out to watch and marvel at the former Princeton All-America. Bill also impressed the Europeans with his scholarliness and wide-ranging interests. Cesare Rubini, the coach of the Simmenthal club, acknowledged of Bradley, "He fulfills the old Greco-Roman traditions of 'a sound mind in a sound body.' "

Early in 1966, Bill was named the Sullivan Award winner for 1965 as America's outstanding amateur athlete for that year, the first time a basketball player was so honored.

Naturally, the New York Knicks were unhappy that Bill had elected to go to Oxford instead of joining them and the NBA. Bradley had time to contemplate his future while in Europe, and finally told the Knicks he would be interested in joining them for the 1967–68 season — if they were still interested in him two years after they had first hoped to sign him. Interested? The Knicks were delighted with Bradley's decision.

He played his first NBA game for the Knicks on December 9, 1967, against the St. Louis Hawks, entering the game to wild applause from the New York fans. He scored 4 points and was generally unimpressive. In his second game, against Detroit, again at Madison Square Garden, he committed a blunder that cost his team the game. With only fifteen seconds to go and New York holding a 2-point lead, he took an unnecessary shot, rather than keep possession of the ball. The shot missed and Detroit scored to tie the game. The Knicks finally lost in overtime.

Whereas Bill had played mostly at forward in college, he spent most of his early days with the Knicks playing at guard. At six feet five, he didn't seem big enough for forward. But at guard, he was often victimized defensively by smaller, quicker players who could easily dribble and drive past him. He concluded his first season as a pro with a scoring average of 8 points per game.

Bradley says he never felt he would be a superstar performer in the pros. "I knew I had weaknesses," he admits. "I never had any aspirations that I was going to score 30 points a game every night. I wanted to become as good a player as I could, and I wanted to contribute to a championship team."

Bill got his chance with the Knicks in his second season with them. One of the regular forwards was injured and Bradley was inserted in his spot. He became a star of a new kind — not a scoring standout, but a superb team player, admired for his intelligence, his uncanny ability to set up plays by moving without the ball, and his tenacious defense. He was one of the necessary players on the team-oriented Knicks who won their first NBA championship in 1969–70. They won again in 1973.

Not all fans recognized Bradley's talents. Totally unselfish, he always concentrated on passing the ball to a teammate who had an open shot. He worked hard to free himself by running crisscross and up-and-down patterns without the ball until his defender grew weary of trying to keep up. Then, with no one around him, he got off unimpeded shots that more often than not swished through the hoop for 2 points.

A ballplayer's ballplayer

Red Holzman, the Knicks' coach, who constantly stressed the team concept of basketball, was the perfect coach for Bradley. "I know there are lots of guys who are stronger, much better rebounders, faster, better on defense, and other things," Holzman says. "But if you threw all the forwards in the NBA into a hat and asked me to pick one, I still think I'd be most happy if I pulled out Bradley's name." (Holzman, incidentally, stepped down as coach of the Knicks at the same time that Bradley retired as a player.)

Instead of relaxing, as many players do, during the basketball off-seasons, Bradley worked hard. "I worked one summer for the Office of Economic Opportunity in Washington, D.C.," he says. "My boss was Donald Rumsfeld, who later became secretary of defense."

Throughout his career Bill has refused to do commercials or to endorse products or services. Most of the top players use commercials as a source of outside income. It is possible for a player to spend a day filming a TV commercial and make as much as $30,000 by the time the commercial has run its course. For simply appearing at a luncheon, a top athlete can earn $2,500. He doesn't have to make a speech, just converse with the other guests.

Bradley declines these opportunities. "Playing for money compromised me enough," he says. "Taking money for hocking products would demean my experience of the game. To me, the advertising industry creates socially useless personal needs and then sells a product to meet those needs. It's not something I want to get involved in."

Prison reform has been a burning issue with Bill for several years. He recalls having an interest in the psychology of prison life even when he was attending Princeton. His interest grew when he was asked to visit a penitentiary in New Jersey shortly after joining the Knicks.

Now he makes regular visits to jails to observe the way they operate, to talk to inmates and prison guards, and to ask questions. He is concerned with rehabilitation programs for inmates, reform of the justice system in the U.S. and of the parole system.

Bradley is a board member of the South Forty Corporation Foundation in New York which develops college equivalency courses and other study materials for prison inmates. He also serves the Wildcat Corporation whose functions include lining up employment for ex-convicts. He even co-produced a Broadway play about prison life. It was *The Poison Tree*, by Robert Ribman, a noted American playwright, and starred Cleavon Little and Moses Gunn, two esteemed black actors.

All this makes Bradley seem more serious and solemn than he is. His teammates on the Knicks learned to expect gags and parodies from him poking fun at himself and others. He delivered the funniest lines with the straightest face — except perhaps for his left eyebrow, which had a habit of arching upward halfway to his hairline. He liked to compare his eyebrow effect to that of Vincent Price, star of many horror films.

In January 1974 he was married to Ernestine Schlant, a professor of German and author of a widely used German textbook. His approach to his own wedding typifies Bradley's concern for privacy. During the All-Star Game break in the NBA schedule, he and Ernestine slipped off by themselves and were married. Although the two had known each other for many months, the marriage came as a complete surprise to Bradley's teammates on the Knicks. Even his roommate didn't know about it until after the wedding.

Bradley wrote his own book about his career in basketball. He didn't just tell his story to a sportswriter as many sports personalities have done. He wrote every word himself. Called *Life on the Run*, it was published in 1976.

Looking to the future, Bill says he may one day run for office in New Jersey where he has lived for most of his years with the Knicks. He has already worked with local leaders helping out with campaigns and legislative proposals.

Bradley is certainly one of the most interesting people in all of sport. The public's interest in him as a basketball player has enabled him to gain a following that will be a great help in any political work he does in the future. "Being well known definitely opens doors for you," he says. Of course, long-term success in politics requires more than a recognizable face. And Bradley's fans needn't think that he will rely on his celebrity alone. His intelligence, determination, and capacity for hard work seem likely to take him almost anywhere he wants to go.

PHOTO CREDITS

B & L Photographers, 55; Camera 5, 34, 42; Cappy Productions, 94, 99; Duomo/Steven E. Sutton, 120, 125, 127, 129, 134; Family Weekly, 88; Michigan State University Photographic Laboratory, 165; United States Air Force, 18; United Press International, 2, 38, 48, 62, 150; White House Official Photograph, 85.

LARRY BORTSTEIN has been a full-time free-lance sports writer since 1969. After graduating from City College of New York, he covered sports for AP and UPI. Since then he has become a contributing editor of *Family Weekly's* national Sunday supplement and writes extensively for other national magazines. Author of more than fifteen sports books— *Ali*, a biography of the boxing champ, is his most recent for young people. Mr. Bortstein loves to collect sports books of all varieties. A New Yorker all his life, Larry Bortstein recently moved to Denver with his wife and their young son.